Publications International, Ltd.

Copyright © 2024 Publications International, Ltd.

All rights reserved. This publication may not be reproduced or quoted in whole or in part by any means whatsoever without written permission from:

Louis Weber, CEO
Publications International, Ltd.
8140 Lehigh Ave
Morton Grove, IL 60053

Permission is never granted for commercial purposes.

Art on cover and throughout copyright © Shutterstock.com.

Pictured on the front cover: Buffalo Cauliflower Bites *(page 76)*.

Pictured on the back cover *(top to bottom):* Roasted Tomato Quiche *(page 16)*, Lentil Ragù *(page 116)* and Devil's Food Sheet Cake *(page 164)*.

ISBN: 978-1-63938-608-6

Manufactured in China.

8 7 6 5 4 3 2 1

Microwave Cooking: Microwave ovens vary in wattage. Use the cooking times as guidelines and check for doneness before adding more time.

WARNING: Food preparation, baking and cooking involve inherent dangers: misuse of electric products, sharp electric tools, boiling water, hot stoves, allergic reactions, foodborne illnesses and the like, pose numerous potential risks. Publications International, Ltd. (PIL) assumes no responsibility or liability for any damages you may experience as a result of following recipes, instructions, tips or advice in this publication.

While we hope this publication helps you find new ways to eat delicious foods, you may not always achieve the results desired due to variations in ingredients, cooking temperatures, typos, errors, omissions or individual cooking abilities.

Let's get social!

 @Publications_International

 @PublicationsInternational

www.pilbooks.com

Contents

BREAKFAST 4

SANDWICHES & PIZZA 34

SNACKS 60

ENTRÉES 90

PASTA 114

SIDES & CASSEROLES 134

SWEETS 162

INDEX 188

Refrigerated biscuits turn into a surprising and fun weekend breakfast in mini monkey breads.

Breakfast

BREAKFAST SAUSAGE MONKEY MUFFINS
MAKES 8 MUFFINS

- 8 ounces bulk pork sausage
- 1 egg, beaten
- 1 cup (4 ounces) shredded Mexican cheese blend, divided
- 1 package (12 ounces) refrigerated buttermilk biscuits (10 biscuits)

1. Preheat oven to 350°F. Spray 8 standard (2½-inch) muffin cups with nonstick cooking spray.

2. Cook sausage in large skillet over medium-high heat 8 minutes or until no longer pink, breaking up meat with spoon. Spoon sausage and drippings into large bowl; let cool 2 minutes. Add egg; stir until blended. Reserve 2 tablespoons cheese for tops of muffins; stir remaining cheese into sausage mixture.

3. Separate biscuits; cut each biscuit into six pieces with scissors. Roll biscuit pieces in sausage mixture to coat; place seven to eight biscuit pieces in each muffin cup. Sprinkle with reserved 2 tablespoons cheese.

4. Bake 22 minutes or until golden brown. Remove muffins to paper towel-lined plate. Serve warm.

Breakfast

PUMPKIN GRANOLA
MAKES ABOUT 5½ CUPS

- 3 cups old-fashioned oats
- ¾ cup coarsely chopped almonds
- ¾ cup raw pepitas (pumpkin seeds)
- ½ cup canned pumpkin
- ½ cup maple syrup
- ⅓ cup coconut oil, melted
- 1 teaspoon ground cinnamon
- 1 teaspoon vanilla
- ½ teaspoon salt
- ¼ teaspoon ground ginger
- ¼ teaspoon ground nutmeg
- Pinch ground cloves
- ¾ cup dried cranberries

1. Preheat oven to 325°F. Line large rimmed baking sheet with parchment paper.

2. Combine oats, almonds and pepitas in large bowl. Combine pumpkin, maple syrup, oil, cinnamon, vanilla, salt, ginger, nutmeg and cloves in medium bowl; stir until well blended. Pour over oat mixture; stir until well blended and all ingredients are completely coated. Spread evenly on prepared baking sheet.

3. Bake 50 to 60 minutes or until granola is golden brown and dry, stirring every 20 minutes. (Granola will become more crisp as it cools.) Stir in cranberries; cool completely.

Variations

For Pumpkin Chocolate Granola, reduce amount of maple syrup to ⅓ cup. Stir in ¾ cup semisweet chocolate chips after baking. You can substitute pecans or walnuts for the almonds, and/or add ¾ cup flaked coconut to the mixture before baking.

Canned pumpkin and pumpkin seeds elevate traditional granola.

Breakfast

CINNAMON-SUGAR WAFFLED BAGELS
MAKES 1 SERVING

- 2 tablespoons butter, softened
- 2 tablespoons packed brown sugar
- 1 teaspoon ground cinnamon
- 1 plain bagel, split

1. Preheat waffle maker to medium; lightly coat with nonstick cooking spray.
2. Combine butter, brown sugar and cinnamon in small bowl. Place bagel halves in waffle maker, close. Press down to flatten slightly; cook 2 minutes or until lightly golden. Remove to plate.
3. Top with butter mixture. Serve warm.

Bagels are the secret to these super easy waffles.

Breakfast

TWISTY CINNAMON FRENCH TOAST
MAKES 4 SERVINGS

- 2 eggs
- ½ cup milk
- ¼ cup maple syrup, plus additional for serving
- 1 teaspoon ground cinnamon
- 2 packages (3 ounces each) ramen noodles*
- 1 tablespoon butter

Use any flavor; discard seasoning packet.

1. Whisk eggs, milk, ¼ cup maple syrup and cinnamon in medium bowl until well blended; pour into 13×9-inch glass baking dish. Carefully break each noodle block into two rectangles. Place in egg mixture; turn to coat both sides. Let stand 30 minutes to soften, turning once.

2. Melt butter in large skillet over medium heat. Add noodle pieces; cook 3 minutes per side until golden brown.

3. Cut noodle pieces in half diagonally; serve with additional syrup.

Move over bread, the secret is out: ramen noodles make amazing French toast!

Breakfast

FRUITY WHOLE-GRAIN CEREAL
MAKES 4 SERVINGS

- 2 cups water
- ½ teaspoon salt
- ¼ cup uncooked quick-cooking pearl barley
- ¼ cup uncooked instant brown rice or whole grain brown rice
- ½ cup milk or almond milk
- ⅓ cup golden raisins
- ¼ cup finely chopped dried dates
- ¼ cup chopped dried plums
- ¼ cup old-fashioned oats
- ¼ cup oat bran
- 2 tablespoons packed brown sugar
- ½ teaspoon ground cinnamon

1. Bring water and salt to a boil in medium saucepan. Add barley and rice. Reduce heat to low; cover and simmer 8 minutes.

2. Stir in milk, raisins, dates, plums, oats, oat bran, brown sugar and cinnamon. Cover and simmer 10 minutes or until mixture is creamy and grains are al dente, stirring once. Serve hot. Refrigerate any leftover cereal in airtight container.

Tip

To reheat cereal, place one serving in microwavable bowl. Microwave 30 seconds; stir. Add water or milk to reach desired consistency. Microwave just until hot.

Multiple grains elevate oatmeal beyond the ordinary.

Breakfast

GRAHAM PANCAKES
MAKES 10 PANCAKES

- 1 cup white cake mix with pudding in the mix
- ¾ cup graham cracker crumbs
- ⅓ cup all-purpose flour
- 1½ teaspoons baking powder
- ½ teaspoon ground cinnamon
- 1½ cups buttermilk*
- 1 egg
- 3 tablespoons butter, melted
- Additional butter (optional)
- Boysenberry or maple syrup (optional)

If buttermilk is unavailable, substitute 4½ teaspoons vinegar or lemon juice and enough milk to equal 1½ cups. Let stand 5 minutes.

1. Preheat oven to 200°F. Place wire rack on baking sheet; place in oven. Heat griddle or large nonstick skillet over medium-low heat; spray with nonstick cooking spray.

2. Whisk cake mix, graham cracker crumbs, flour, baking powder and cinnamon in large bowl. Whisk buttermilk, egg and melted butter in medium bowl. Add to dry ingredients; mix until smooth.

3. Drop batter by ⅓ cupfuls about 2 inches apart onto griddle. Cook 3 to 4 minutes or until bubbles appear on top. Turn over; cook 2 minutes longer or until bottoms are golden brown. Transfer to wire rack on baking sheet in oven to keep warm. Repeat with remaining batter. Serve with butter and syrup, if desired.

Graham cracker crumbs are an unexpected addition to regular pancakes.

Breakfast

ROASTED TOMATO QUICHE
MAKES 6 SERVINGS

- 1 pint grape tomatoes
- 1 tablespoon olive oil
- Salt and black pepper
- 2½ cups riced cauliflower (fresh or frozen)*
- ½ cup shredded Parmesan cheese
- 6 eggs, divided
- ¾ teaspoon salt, divided
- ½ teaspoon black pepper, divided
- ¾ cup milk
- ½ cup (2 ounces) shredded mozzarella cheese
- 2 cloves garlic, minced
- ½ teaspoon fresh thyme leaves

*To make riced cauliflower, cut one head of cauliflower into 1-inch florets. Working in batches, pulse the florets until they form small rice-size pieces. If there are any large chunks left behind, pick them out and add them to your next batch. Or grate a whole head of cauliflower on the large holes of a box grater into a large bowl, rotating until all the florets are shredded.

1. Preheat oven to 350°F. Place tomatoes in shallow baking dish; drizzle with oil and sprinkle lightly with salt and pepper. Bake 1 hour, stirring once or twice.**

2. Spray 9-inch pie plate with nonstick cooking spray. Place cauliflower in large microwavable bowl; cover with plastic wrap and cut slit to vent. Microwave on HIGH 4 minutes; stir. Cover and cook on HIGH 4 minutes. Remove cover; cool slightly. Place cauliflower on double layer of paper towels; fold over paper towels and squeeze to remove excess moisture. Return to bowl. Add Parmesan cheese, 1 egg, ½ teaspoon salt and ¼ teaspoon pepper; mix well. Press onto bottom and up side of prepared pie plate. *Increase oven temperature to 425°F.* Bake crust 15 minutes. Remove from oven; place on baking sheet.

3. *Reduce oven temperature to 375°F.* Whisk 5 eggs, milk, mozzarella cheese, garlic, thyme, remaining ¼ teaspoon salt and ¼ teaspoon pepper in medium bowl until well blended. Place tomatoes in crust; pour egg mixture over tomatoes.

4. Bake 45 minutes or until thin knife inserted into center comes out clean (a little cheese is okay). Cool 10 minutes before slicing.

**Tomatoes can be roasted a day in advance.

Cauliflower and cheese make a low-carb and delicious crust for quiche.

Breakfast

MARBLED BANANA BREAD
MAKES 10 TO 12 SERVINGS

- 2 cups all-purpose flour
- 1 teaspoon baking soda
- 1 teaspoon salt
- 1 cup sugar
- 6 tablespoons (¾ stick) butter, softened
- 1½ cups mashed ripe bananas (about 3 medium)
- 2 eggs
- ½ cup sour cream
- 1 teaspoon vanilla
- ¾ cup semisweet or bittersweet chocolate chips

1. Preheat oven to 350°F. Spray 9×5-inch loaf pan with nonstick cooking spray or line with parchment paper.

2. Whisk flour, baking soda and salt in medium bowl. Beat sugar and butter in large bowl with wooden spoon until well blended. Add bananas, eggs, sour cream and vanilla; stir until blended. Add flour mixture; stir just until dry ingredients are moistened.

3. Place chocolate chips in medium microwavable bowl; microwave on HIGH 1 minute. Stir until chocolate is melted and smooth; let cool 3 minutes. Add 1 cup batter to melted chocolate; stir until well blended. Spoon plain and chocolate batters alternately into prepared pan; swirl batters together with knife or wooden skewer.

4. Bake 1 hour to 1 hour 5 minutes or until toothpick inserted into center comes out clean. Cool in pan 10 minutes. Remove to wire rack; cool completely.

Chocolate is the secret to amazing banana bread.

Breakfast

BACON AND EGG BREAKFAST CASSEROLE
MAKES 6 SERVINGS

CRUST

- 2 cups riced cauliflower (fresh or frozen)*
- ½ cup shredded Parmesan cheese
- 1 egg
- ¼ teaspoon salt
- ⅛ teaspoon ground red pepper (optional)

FILLING

- 1 package (about 12 ounces) bacon, chopped
- 1 onion, chopped
- 1 jalapeño pepper, seeded and chopped
- 2 cloves garlic, minced
- 1 cup (4 ounces) shredded Cheddar cheese, divided
- 8 eggs
- ¾ cup milk
- ¼ teaspoon salt

See note on page 16.

1. Preheat oven to 400°F. Place cauliflower in large microwavable bowl; cover with plastic wrap and cut slit to vent. Microwave on HIGH 4 minutes; stir. Cover and cook on HIGH 4 minutes. Remove cover; cool slightly. Place cauliflower on double layer of paper towels; fold over paper towels and squeeze to remove excess moisture. Return to bowl. Add Parmesan cheese, 1 egg, ¼ teaspoon salt and red pepper, if desired; mix well. Press onto bottom and up side of 8-inch square baking pan. Bake 15 minutes. Remove from oven. *Reduce oven temperature to 350°F.*

2. Meanwhile, cook and stir bacon in large skillet over medium heat until crisp. Remove to paper towel-lined plate with slotted spoon. Reserve ¼ cup bacon for top of casserole; set aside.

3. Drain all but 1 tablespoon drippings from skillet; heat skillet over medium heat. Add onion; cook and stir 5 minutes or until onion is softened. Add jalapeño and garlic; cook and stir 30 seconds. Remove from heat. Place onion mixture and bacon in crust; sprinkle with ¾ cup Cheddar cheese.

4. Whisk 8 eggs, milk and ¼ teaspoon salt in large bowl until well blended. Pour into crust.

5. Bake 30 minutes. Sprinkle with remaining ¼ cup Cheddar cheese and reserved bacon; bake 5 minutes or until cheese is melted. Cut into six squares.

Cauliflower is even better than potatoes in this bacony egg and cheese breakfast.

Breakfast

THREE-INGREDIENT BAGELS
MAKES 4 BAGELS

- 1¼ cups self-rising flour
- 1 cup plain Greek yogurt
- 1 egg, beaten
- Sesame seeds, poppy seeds, dried onion flakes and/or everything bagel seasoning (optional)
- Cream cheese or butter (optional)

1. Preheat oven to 400°F. Line baking sheet with parchment paper.

2. Attach dough hook to electric mixer. Combine flour and yogurt in mixer bowl. Knead at medium-low speed 2 minutes or until mixture is well combined.* Turn out dough onto lightly floured surface; knead 3 minutes or until dough is smooth and elastic but slightly tacky. Shape dough into a ball.

3. Cut into four equal pieces; roll into balls. Poke finger though center of balls, stretching into bagel shapes (make large exaggerated loops; they will close up while baking). Place bagels on prepared baking sheet; brush with egg. Sprinkle with desired toppings.

4. Bake 15 to 20 minutes or until lightly browned. Serve warm with cream cheese, if desired.

*Or use heavy spatula in large bowl to combine mixture.

Self-rising flour and Greek yogurt magically make easy bagels.

Breakfast

QUINOA BREAKFAST FRIED "RICE"
MAKES 4 SERVINGS

- 1 cup uncooked quinoa
- 1½ cups water
- ¼ teaspoon plus ⅛ teaspoon salt, divided
- 2 tablespoons vegetable oil, divided
- 1 carrot, finely diced
- ¾ cup peas
- 4 ounces deli ham, finely diced (optional)
- 2 green onions, thinly sliced
- 2 teaspoons minced garlic
- 1 teaspoon grated ginger
- 3 eggs, lightly beaten
- 1 tablespoon soy sauce, plus additional for serving
- 1 tablespoon ketchup
- ¼ teaspoon freshly ground black pepper

1. Place quinoa in fine-mesh strainer; rinse well under cold water. Combine quinoa, 1½ cups water and ¼ teaspoon salt in large saucepan; bring to a boil over medium-high heat. Reduce heat to low; cover and cook about 15 minutes or until quinoa is tender and water is absorbed. Spread on baking sheet; cool completely.

2. Heat 1 tablespoon oil in large nonstick skillet over medium-high heat. Add carrot and peas; cook and stir about 4 minutes or until softened. Add ham, if desired; cook about 2 minutes or until lightly browned. Add green onions, garlic and ginger; cook about 1 minute or until fragrant. Transfer to large bowl.

3. Heat remaining 1 tablespoon oil in skillet over medium-high heat. Add eggs and remaining ⅛ teaspoon salt; cook about 1 minute or until lightly scrambled and set. Break up eggs into small, bite-size pieces with spatula.

4. Return carrot mixture to skillet. Add quinoa; cook and stir 2 minutes. Add 1 tablespoon soy sauce, ketchup and pepper; cook and stir 1 minute or until heated through. Serve with additional soy sauce, if desired.

Tip

To save time in the morning, prepare the quinoa the night before and refrigerate, then begin with step 2.

Healthy high-protein quinoa replaces rice.

Breakfast

BAKED PUMPKIN OATMEAL
MAKES 6 SERVINGS

- 2 cups old-fashioned oats
- 2 cups milk
- 1 cup canned pumpkin
- 2 eggs
- ⅓ cup packed brown sugar
- 1 teaspoon vanilla
- ½ cup dried cranberries, plus additional for serving
- 1 teaspoon pumpkin pie spice
- ½ teaspoon salt
- ½ teaspoon baking powder
- Maple syrup
- Chopped pecans (optional)

1. Preheat oven to 350°F. Spray 8-inch square baking dish with nonstick cooking spray.

2. Spread oats on ungreased baking sheet. Bake 10 minutes or until fragrant and lightly browned, stirring occasionally. Pour into medium bowl; let cool slightly.

3. Whisk milk, pumpkin, eggs, brown sugar and vanilla in large bowl until well blended. Add ½ cup cranberries, pumpkin pie spice, salt and baking powder to oats; mix well. Add oat mixture to pumpkin mixture; stir until well blended. Pour into prepared baking dish.

4. Bake 45 minutes or until set and knife inserted into center comes out almost clean. Serve warm with maple syrup, additional cranberries and pecans, if desired.

Canned pumpkin is the healthy secret to delicious oatmeal.

Breakfast

BANANA BREAD WAFFLES WITH CINNAMON BUTTER
MAKES 4 SERVINGS

- ½ cup whipped butter, softened
- 2 tablespoons powdered sugar
- 2 teaspoons grated orange peel
- ¼ teaspoon ground cinnamon
- ¼ teaspoon vanilla
- 1 package (7 ounces) banana muffin mix
- ⅔ cup buttermilk
- 1 egg
- Maple syrup

1. Preheat waffle maker.
2. Combine butter, powdered sugar, orange peel, cinnamon and vanilla in small bowl; mix well.
3. Combine muffin mix, buttermilk and egg in medium bowl; stir until just moistened.
4. Spray waffle maker with nonstick cooking spray. Spoon half of batter (1 cup) onto waffle maker and cook according to manufacturer's directions. Repeat with remaining batter.
5. Serve waffles with butter mixture and maple syrup.

Banana muffin mix makes the easiest three-ingredient waffles.

Breakfast

CHERRY SCONES WITH STRAWBERRY BUTTER
MAKES 12 SCONES

SCONES

- 2 cups biscuit baking mix
- 2 tablespoons sugar
- 1 teaspoon grated lemon peel
- ⅓ cup milk or whipping cream
- ¼ cup dried cherries
- 1 egg, separated
- 1 teaspoon water

FRUIT SPREAD

- ½ cup (1 stick) butter, softened
- ¼ cup strawberry fruit spread
- ½ teaspoon vanilla

1. Preheat oven to 400°F. Spray large baking sheet with nonstick cooking spray.

2. Stir together baking mix, sugar, lemon peel, milk, cherries and egg yolk in medium bowl. Shape dough into a ball. Pat or roll out to ½-inch thickness on floured work surface. Cut out scones with 2-inch biscuit cutter. Gather scraps and reroll as necessary. Place scones on baking sheet.

3. Whisk egg white and water in small bowl until well blended. Brush evenly over scones. Bake 10 minutes.

4. Meanwhile, stir butter, fruit spread and vanilla in small bowl until well blended. Serve with warm scones.

Biscuit baking mix makes quick work of scones.

Breakfast

EGG AND GREEN CHILE RICE CASSEROLE
MAKES 4 SERVINGS

- ¾ cup uncooked instant brown rice
- ½ cup chopped green onions
- ½ teaspoon ground cumin
- 1 can (4 ounces) diced mild green chiles, drained
- ⅛ teaspoon salt
- 1 cup liquid egg substitute
- ½ cup (2 ounces) shredded sharp Cheddar cheese or Mexican cheese blend
- ¼ cup pico de gallo
- Lime wedges

1. Preheat oven to 350°F. Lightly spray 8-inch square baking dish with nonstick cooking spray.
2. Cook rice according to package directions. Stir in green onions and cumin. Spread mixture in prepared baking dish.
3. Sprinkle chiles and salt evenly over rice mixture. Pour egg substitute evenly over top.
4. Bake 30 to 35 minutes or until center is set. Sprinkle with cheese; bake 3 minutes or until cheese is melted. Let stand 5 minutes before cutting into four squares. Serve with pico de gallo and lime wedges.

Convenience products (instant brown rice and egg substitute) make an easy breakfast bake.

Grilled cheese gets an upgrade with the addition of grilled vegetables.

Sandwiches & Pizza

VEGETABLE AND CHEESE SANDWICHES
MAKES 2 SERVINGS

- 1 large zucchini, cut lengthwise into ¼-inch slices
- 2 slices sweet onion (¼ inch thick)
- 1 yellow bell pepper, cut lengthwise into quarters
- 4 tablespoons Caesar salad dressing, divided
- 4 slices sourdough bread
- 4 slices (1 ounce each) Muenster cheese
- 2 slices (1 ounce each) Swiss or Gouda cheese

1. Prepare grill for direct cooking.* Brush vegetables with 2 tablespoons dressing. Place vegetables on grid over medium coals. Grill on covered grill 5 minutes. Turn; grill 2 minutes.

2. Brush both sides of bread lightly with remaining 2 tablespoons dressing. Place bread around vegetables; grill 2 minutes or until bread is lightly toasted. Turn bread; top each slice with one slice of Muenster cheese and two slices with slice of Swiss cheese. Grill vegetables and bread 1 to 2 minutes more or until cheese is melted, bread is toasted and vegetables are crisp-tender.

3. Arrange vegetables over slices of bread with Swiss cheese; top with remaining bread.

*To make this sandwich without a grill, cook vegetables in grill pan or cast iron skillet until vegetables are browned and tender.

Sandwiches & Pizza

GARLIC AND ONION SHEET PAN PIZZA
MAKES 6 SERVINGS

- 2 teaspoons vegetable oil
- 1 head cauliflower (1½ pounds)
- ¾ cup almond flour
- ½ cup shredded Parmesan cheese
- 1½ cups (6 ounces) shredded mozzarella cheese, divided
- 1 teaspoon salt
- 1 clove garlic
- ½ teaspoon dried oregano
- Black pepper
- 1 egg
- 1 cup prepared Indian butter chicken sauce*
- ½ sweet onion, halved and thinly sliced
- 1 tablespoon chopped garlic
- Torn fresh basil leaves (optional)

*Or stir ¼ cup whipping cream into 1 cup prepared marinara sauce in small bowl.

1. Preheat oven to 425°F. Grease large baking sheet with oil.

2. Break cauliflower into florets. Working in batches, pulse cauliflower in food processor until finely chopped (or grate on the large holes of a box grater). Measure 4 cups; place in large bowl. Reserve remaining cauliflower for another use. Add almond flour, Parmesan cheese, ½ cup mozzarella cheese, salt, 1 clove garlic and oregano. Season with black pepper; mix well. Add egg; mix with hands until thoroughly blended. Turn out onto prepared baking sheet; pat into 11×14-inch rectangle. Bake 20 minutes.

3. Remove crust from oven. Spread sauce over crust to within ½ inch of edges. Sprinkle evenly with onion, chopped garlic and remaining 1 cup mozzarella cheese.

4. Bake 7 to 10 minutes or until cheese is bubbly and browned in spots. Sprinkle with basil, if desired. Cut into squares to serve.

Indian butter chicken sauce makes a great creamy, lightly spiced pizza sauce.

Sandwiches & Pizza

CHORIZO QUESADILLAS
MAKES 6 SERVINGS

- 1 package (9 ounces) regular or vegetarian chorizo
- 1 cup coarsely chopped cauliflower
- 1 small onion, finely chopped
- 12 (6-inch) flour tortillas
- 1½ cups (6 ounces) chihuahua cheese
- 6 teaspoons vegetable oil
- Salsa, guacamole and sour cream

1. Heat medium skillet over medium-high heat. Add chorizo, cauliflower and onion; cook and stir 10 to 12 minutes or until cauliflower is tender. Transfer to bowl. Wipe out skillet.

2. Spread ¼ cup chorizo mixture onto each of six tortillas. Top with ¼ cup cheese and remaining tortillas.

3. Heat 1 teaspoon oil in same skillet over medium-high heat. Add one quesadilla; cook 2 to 3 minutes per side or until well browned and cheese is melted. Repeat with remaining oil and quesadillas. Cut into wedges; serve with salsa, guacamole and sour cream.

Note

To keep cooked quesadillas warm, arrange on a baking sheet and place in a preheated 200°F oven until all the quesadillas are cooked.

Cauliflower adds an unexpected twist to hearty quesadillas.

Sandwiches & Pizza

BBQ PORTOBELLOS
MAKES 4 SERVINGS

- 1 teaspoon salt
- 1 teaspoon smoked paprika
- 1 teaspoon onion powder
- ½ teaspoon garlic powder
- ½ teaspoon ground cumin
- ½ teaspoon black pepper
- 4 portobello mushroom caps
- 2 tablespoons plus 1 teaspoon olive oil, divided
- ½ medium yellow onion, finely chopped
- ¼ cup ketchup
- 2 tablespoons apple cider vinegar
- 1 tablespoon Dijon mustard
- 1 tablespoon packed brown sugar
- 1 teaspoon soy sauce
- 4 hamburger buns
- Mayonnaise, sliced dill pickles and/or shredded cabbage or lettuce

1. Preheat oven to 375°F. Line baking sheet with parchment paper.
2. Combine salt, paprika, onion powder, garlic powder, cumin and pepper in small bowl. Scrape gills from mushrooms and remove any stems. Cut mushrooms into ½-inch slices; place in large bowl. Drizzle with 2 tablespoons oil; toss to coat. Add seasoning mixture; toss until well blended. Arrange slices in single layer on prepared baking sheet.
3. Bake 15 minutes. Turn and bake 5 minutes or until mushrooms are tender and have shrunken slightly.
4. Meanwhile, heat remaining 1 teaspoon oil in small saucepan over medium-high heat. Add onion; cook and stir 5 minutes or until onion is very soft. Add ketchup, vinegar, mustard, brown sugar and soy sauce; mix well. Reduce heat to low; simmer 5 minutes. Combine mushrooms and sauce in large bowl; mix well. Serve on buns with mayonnaise, pickles and cabbage.

Tip

For a smooth sauce, process sauce in mini food processor or blender until smooth.

Sandwiches & Pizza

MARGHERITA PIZZA WITH QUINOA CRUST
MAKES 4 SERVINGS

- 1 cup uncooked quinoa
- ⅓ cup water, plus additional for soaking
- 1 tablespoon olive oil, plus drizzle for serving
- 1 teaspoon baking powder
- ¾ teaspoon kosher salt
- ½ cup marinara sauce
- 1 ball (8 ounces) fresh mozzarella cheese, cut into ¼-inch-thick slices
- Slivered fresh basil leaves, flaky sea salt and black pepper (optional)

1. Place quinoa in medium bowl; cover with 1 inch of water. Cover; let stand 8 hours or overnight at room temperature.

2. Preheat oven to 450°F. Line bottom of 10-inch springform pan with foil. Brush with 1 tablespoon oil. Attach sides of pan.

3. Rinse and drain quinoa. Place quinoa, ⅓ cup water, baking powder and kosher salt in bowl of food processor. Process 2 minutes or until completely smooth, stopping occasionally to scrape down sides of bowl as needed. Spread quinoa mixture evenly in prepared pan. Bake 10 to 12 minutes or until quinoa is golden.

4. Remove pan from oven. Remove sides of pan. Spread marinara sauce evenly over crust. Top with cheese; return to oven. Bake 10 minutes or until cheese is melted and bottom of crust is golden brown.

5. Slide pizza onto large cutting board. Top with basil and drizzle with additional oil. Sprinkle with sea salt and pepper, if desired. Slice and serve immediately.

Soaked quinoa makes a crispy gluten-free pizza crust.

Sandwiches & Pizza

TURKEY DINNER QUESADILLA
MAKES 1 SERVING

- 1 large (10- to 12-inch) flour tortilla
- 2 slices deli turkey
- 2 slices (1 ounce each) Swiss cheese
- 2 tablespoons whole berry cranberry sauce
- ¼ cup baby spinach

1. Lay tortilla on flat surface. Cut one slit from outer edge of tortilla to center.

2. Place turkey slices, cheese slices, cranberry sauce and spinach in each of the four quadrants of tortilla. Beginning with the cut edge, fold the tortilla in quarters, covering each quadrant until you have the entire quesadilla folded into one large triangle. Spray outside of quesadilla with nonstick cooking spray.

3. Heat small skillet over medium heat; spray with cooking spray. Add quesadilla; cook 3 to 5 minutes per side or until tortilla is lightly browned and cheese is melted.

Cranberry sauce turns a regular quesadilla into a leftover Thanksgiving treat.

Sandwiches & Pizza

ALMOND CHICKEN SALAD SANDWICH
MAKES 4 SERVINGS

- ¼ cup mayonnaise
- ¼ cup plain Greek yogurt or sour cream
- 2 tablespoons cider vinegar
- 1 tablespoon honey
- 1 teaspoon salt
- ½ teaspoon black pepper
- ⅛ teaspoon garlic powder
- 2 cups chopped cooked chicken
- ¾ cup halved red grapes
- 1 stalk celery, chopped
- ⅓ cup sliced almonds
- Leaf lettuce
- 1 tomato, thinly sliced
- 8 slices sesame semolina or country Italian bread

1. Whisk mayonnaise, yogurt, vinegar, honey, salt, pepper and garlic powder in small bowl until well blended.

2. Combine chicken, grapes and celery in medium bowl. Add dressing; toss gently to coat. Cover and refrigerate several hours or overnight. Stir in almonds just before making sandwiches.

3. Place lettuce and tomato slices on four bread slices; top with chicken salad and remaining bread slices. Serve immediately.

Grapes are the perfect sweet-tart addition to classic chicken salad.

Sandwiches & Pizza

HEARTY VEGGIE SANDWICH
MAKES 4 SERVINGS

- 1 pound cremini mushrooms, stemmed and thinly sliced (⅛-inch slices)
- 2 tablespoons olive oil, divided
- ¾ teaspoon salt, divided
- ¼ teaspoon black pepper
- 1 medium zucchini, diced (¼-inch pieces, about 2 cups)
- 3 tablespoons butter, softened
- 8 slices whole grain or whole wheat bread
- ¼ cup pesto sauce
- ¼ cup mayonnaise
- 2 cups packed baby spinach
- 4 slices (1 ounce each) mozzarella cheese

1. Preheat oven to 350°F. Combine mushrooms, 1 tablespoon oil, ½ teaspoon salt and pepper in medium bowl; toss to coat. Spread in single layer on large rimmed baking sheet. Roast 20 minutes or until mushrooms are dark brown and dry, stirring after 10 minutes. Cool on baking sheet.

2. Meanwhile, heat remaining 1 tablespoon oil in large skillet over medium heat. Add zucchini and remaining ¼ teaspoon salt; cook and stir 5 minutes or until zucchini is tender and lightly browned. Remove to medium bowl; wipe out skillet with paper towels.

3. Spread butter on one side of each bread slice. Turn over slices. Spread pesto on four bread slices; spread mayonnaise on remaining four slices. Top pesto-covered slices evenly with mushrooms; layer with spinach, zucchini and cheese. Top with remaining bread slices, mayonnaise side down.

4. Heat same skillet over medium heat. Add sandwiches; cover and cook 2 minutes per side or until bread is toasted, spinach is slightly wilted and cheese is beginning to melt. Serve immediately.

Pesto is the secret to a super delicious sandwich.

Sandwiches & Pizza

BAVARIAN PRETZEL SANDWICHES
MAKES 4 SANDWICHES

- 4 frozen soft pretzels, thawed
- 1 tablespoon German mustard
- 2 teaspoons mayonnaise
- 8 slices Black Forest ham
- 4 slices Gouda cheese
- 1 tablespoon water
- Coarse pretzel salt

1. Preheat oven to 350°F. Line baking sheet with parchment paper.

2. Carefully slice each pretzel in half crosswise using serrated knife. Combine mustard and mayonnaise in small bowl. Spread mustard mixture onto bottom halves of pretzels. Top with 2 slices ham, 1 slice cheese and top halves of pretzels.

3. Place sandwiches on prepared baking sheet. Brush tops of sandwiches with water; sprinkle with salt. Bake 8 minutes or until cheese is melted.

Note
For cold sandwiches, bake the pretzels according to package directions. When they are cool enough to handle, slice them and top with the sandwich fillings.

Frozen pretzels are a super fun substitution for pretzel rolls or regular bread.

Sandwiches & Pizza

SUMMER VEGETABLE PIZZA
MAKES 4 SERVINGS

- 1 prepared whole wheat pizza crust (10 ounces)
- 2 large plum tomatoes, thinly sliced
- 2 teaspoons olive oil
- 2 small zucchini, thinly sliced
- 1 small eggplant, peeled and thinly sliced
- ⅓ cup thinly sliced red onion
- 1 teaspoon minced garlic
- ¼ teaspoon salt
- 1 cup (4 ounces) shredded mozzarella cheese
- 1 tablespoon grated Romano cheese
- 3 tablespoons chopped fresh basil

1. Preheat oven to 450°F. Place pizza crust on baking sheet. Arrange tomatoes on crust.

2. Heat oil in large skillet over medium-high heat. Add zucchini, eggplant, onion, garlic and salt; cook and stir 4 to 5 minutes or until zucchini is crisp-tender. Layer vegetables over tomatoes on crust; top with cheeses.

3. Bake 10 to 12 minutes or until cheeses are melted and crust is golden brown. Sprinkle with basil.

Make a mix of summer vegetables your secret for amazing pizza.

Sandwiches & Pizza

VEGGIE-PACKED TURKEY BURGERS
MAKES 4 SERVINGS

- 1 pound ground turkey
- ½ cup shredded onion
- ½ cup shredded zucchini, squeezed dry
- ½ cup shredded carrots
- 1 teaspoon minced jalapeño pepper
- Salt and black pepper
- 4 whole wheat rolls or hamburger buns
- Shredded lettuce and tomato slices

1. Prepare grill for direct cooking over medium-heat. Combine turkey, onion, zucchini, carrots and jalapeño in large bowl. Season with salt and black pepper. Shape into four patties.
2. Grill, covered, 8 to 10 minutes or until cooked through (165°F), turning halfway through grilling.
3. Serve on rolls with lettuce and tomato slices.

Tip

Grate the onion, zucchini and carrots on the large holes of a box grater.

The secret to deliciously moist and flavorful turkey burgers is a mix of shredded vegetables.

Sandwiches & Pizza

VEGETABLE PIZZA PRIMAVERA
MAKES 4 SERVINGS

- ½ cup warm water (110° to 115°F)
- ¾ teaspoon sugar
- ¾ teaspoon active dry yeast
- 1½ cups all-purpose or bread flour, plus additional if needed
- ½ teaspoon salt
- 1½ cups small broccoli florets
- 1 carrot, shredded
- 1 small yellow squash or zucchini, cut into ¼-inch-thick slices
- 6 thin asparagus spears, cut into 1½-inch pieces
- 10 fresh pea pods
- 1 cup (4 ounces) shredded Swiss cheese or provolone cheese
- 1 green onion, thinly sliced
- ⅓ cup slivered fresh basil leaves *or* 2 tablespoons chopped fresh tarragon leaves
- ¼ cup grated Romano cheese
- Black pepper
- 1 teaspoon olive oil

1. Combine ½ cup water, sugar and yeast in medium bowl; stir to dissolve sugar and yeast. Let stand 5 minutes or until foamy. Stir in flour and salt until soft dough forms.

2. Knead dough on lightly floured surface 5 minutes or until dough is smooth and elastic, adding additional flour, 1 tablespoon at a time, as needed. Place dough in large greased bowl; turn to grease top. Cover and let rise in warm place 30 minutes or until doubled in size.

3. Preheat oven to 500°F.

4. Grease large baking sheet. Punch dough down; place on lightly floured surface and shape into a ball. Let rest 2 minutes. Pat and gently stretch dough into 12-inch circle; let dough rest for a few minutes if it is hard to stretch. Place on prepared baking sheet.

5. Bring large saucepan of salted water to a boil. Add broccoli, carrot and asparagus; cook 3 minutes. Add squash, cook 1 minutes. Add pea pods; cook 1 minute. Drain and pat vegetables dry.

6. Sprinkle Swiss cheese over dough, leaving 1-inch border. Bake 3 to 4 minutes or until cheese melts and crust is light golden. Place all vegetables on pizza. Top with basil, Romano cheese and pepper. Bake 4 to 6 minutes or until crust is deep golden and cheese is melted. Brush edge of crust with olive oil.

Tip

The secret to quicker pizza is refrigerated pizza dough. Look for balls of dough near the refrigerated prepared foods in the grocery store. Skip steps 1 and 2 and proceed with step 3.

Broccoli pizza is the most delicious way to get a serving of healthy veggies.

Sandwiches & Pizza

HOT DOG SLOPPY JOE SANDWICHES
MAKES 2 SANDWICHES

- 3 to 4 hot dogs
- 1 tablespoon vegetable oil
- 2 tablespoons barbecue sauce
- 2 hamburger buns or pretzel rolls, split and toasted

1. Cut each hot dog lengthwise into ¼-inch strips (8 to 10 strips per hot dog).

2. Heat oil in large skillet over medium-high heat. Add hot dog strips; cook 5 to 7 minutes or until hot dog strips curl and are lightly browned. Add barbecue sauce; cook and stir 1 minute.

3. Pile hot dog strips in buns. Serve immediately.

The secret to a quick and easy sloppy sandwich is sliced hot dogs.

Cauliflower stands in for shrimp in this sweet-spicy snack.

Snacks

SWEET-SPICY BREADED CAULIFLOWER
MAKES 4 TO 6 SERVINGS

- ½ cup mayonnaise
- ¼ cup sweet chili sauce
- 1½ teaspoons hot pepper sauce
- ¼ teaspoon salt
- ⅛ teaspoon black pepper
- 2 tablespoons water
- ¼ cup all-purpose flour
- 1 cup panko bread crumbs
- 1 head cauliflower, cut into florets
- 2 green onions, chopped

1. Preheat oven to 425°F. Line baking sheet with parchment paper.

2. Combine mayonnaise, chili sauce, hot pepper sauce, salt and black pepper in small bowl. Remove half of mixture; refrigerate until ready to serve. Stir water into remaining mayonnaise mixture. Place flour in large bowl; place panko in shallow dish.

3. Working in batches, coat cauliflower in flour. Dip in sauce mixture one at a time; roll in panko to coat.

4. Bake 30 minutes or until cauliflower is tender and coating is golden brown.

5. Place cauliflower on serving plate; sprinkle with green onions. Serve with reserved sauce mixture.

Snacks

EGGPLANT PIZZAS
MAKES 8 MINI PIZZAS

- 1 egg
- 1 tablespoon water
- ¾ cup seasoned Italian bread crumbs
- 1 medium unpeeled eggplant, sliced into ½-inch rounds
- Olive oil
- ½ cup marinara sauce
- ½ cup (2 ounces) shredded mozzarella cheese
- Chopped fresh basil

1. Preheat oven to 400°F. Line baking sheet with foil; spray foil with nonstick cooking spray.

2. Beat egg and water in shallow dish. Place bread crumbs in another shallow dish. Dip eggplant in egg, letting excess drip back into dish. Coat with bread crumbs, pressing gently to adhere. Place on prepared baking sheet. Drizzle with oil.

3. Bake 20 minutes or until eggplant is tender and coating is golden brown. Remove from oven.

4. Place about 1 tablespoon marinara sauce on top of each eggplant slice. Top with cheese. Bake 5 minutes or until cheese is melted and golden brown. Sprinkle with basil just before serving.

Note
Top pizzas with bell peppers, sliced tomatoes, olives or any other favorite toppings.

Eggplant is a healthy and delicious substitute for pizza crust.

Snacks

MEATBALL SLIDERS
MAKES 24 SLIDERS

- 1 can (15 ounces) whole berry cranberry sauce
- 1 can (about 15 ounces) tomato sauce
- ⅛ teaspoon red pepper flakes (optional)
- 2 pounds ground beef or turkey
- ¾ cup plain dry bread crumbs
- 1 egg
- 1 package (1 ounce) dry onion soup mix
-   Baby arugula or spinach leaves (optional)
- 24 small potato rolls or dinner rolls, split
- 6 slices (1 ounce each) provolone cheese, cut into quarters

1. Preheat oven to 350°F. Combine cranberry sauce, tomato sauce and red pepper flakes, if desired, in medium bowl.

2. Combine beef, bread crumbs, egg and soup mix in large bowl; mix well. Shape mixture into 24 (1¾-inch) meatballs. Place in 13×9-inch baking pan or glass baking dish; pour sauce over meatballs, making sure all meatballs are covered in sauce.

3. Bake 40 to 45 minutes or until meatballs are cooked through (165°F), basting with sauce once or twice during cooking.

4. Place arugula leaves on bottom of rolls, if desired; top with meatballs and cheese. Spoon sauce from pan over meatballs and cover with roll tops.

Cranberry sauce and onion soup mix are a magic sauce combo for mini meatball sandwiches.

Snacks

TUNA ARTICHOKE CUPS
MAKES 12 CUPS

- 1 can (6 ounces) tuna packed in water, preferably albacore, drained, liquid reserved
- ¼ cup minced shallots
- 1 tablespoon white wine vinegar
- ¼ teaspoon ground coriander
- 4 ounces cream cheese, softened
- 1 can (about 14 ounces) artichoke hearts, drained and coarsely chopped
- 1 tablespoon lemon juice
- ½ teaspoon salt
- ¼ teaspoon white pepper
- Dash ground nutmeg
- 12 wonton wrappers
- 2 tablespoons butter, melted

1. Preheat oven to 350°F. Combine reserved tuna liquid, shallots, vinegar and coriander in small saucepan. Bring to a boil over medium-high heat. Reduce heat to low; simmer, uncovered, until liquid has evaporated. Add tuna and cream cheese; cook until cheese melts, stirring constantly. Stir in artichokes, lemon juice, salt, pepper and nutmeg. Cool slightly.

2. Gently press one wonton wrapper into each of 12 standard (2½-inch) muffin cups, allowing ends to extend above edges of cups. Spoon tuna mixture evenly into wonton wrappers.

3. Brush edges of wonton wrappers with melted butter. Bake 20 minutes or until tuna mixture is set and edges of wonton wrappers are browned.

Wonton wrappers make the perfect crust for mini tuna casseroles.

Snacks

SAVORY PUMPKIN HUMMUS
MAKES 1½ CUPS

- 1 can (about 15 ounces) pumpkin purée
- 3 tablespoons chopped fresh parsley, plus additional for garnish
- 3 tablespoons tahini
- 3 tablespoons lemon juice
- 2 cloves garlic
- 1 teaspoon ground cumin
- ½ teaspoon salt
- ⅛ teaspoon black pepper
- ⅛ teaspoon ground red pepper, plus additional for garnish
- Assorted vegetable sticks

1. Combine pumpkin, 3 tablespoons parsley, tahini, lemon juice, garlic, cumin, salt, black pepper and ⅛ teaspoon ground red pepper in food processor or blender; process until smooth.
2. Place in serving bowl; cover and refrigerate at least 2 hours to allow flavors to develop.
3. Sprinkle with additional ground red pepper, if desired. Garnish with additional parsley. Serve with vegetables.

Instead of chickpeas, try pumpkin in your next hummus.

Snacks

WING-STYLE FRIED MUSHROOMS
MAKES 2 TO 4 SERVINGS

- 2 teaspoons garlic powder
- 1½ teaspoons paprika
- 1½ teaspoons poultry seasoning
- 1 teaspoon onion powder
- ½ teaspoon celery seed
- ½ teaspoon chili powder
- ½ teaspoon ground sage
- ½ teaspoon dried thyme
- ¾ cup panko bread crumbs
- ½ cup all-purpose flour
- 1 cup buttermilk
- 2 tablespoons hot pepper sauce
- 4 ounces oyster mushrooms, cut into 1- to 2-inch pieces (2 cups)
- Vegetable oil for frying
- Blue cheese dressing and celery and carrot sticks

1. Combine garlic powder, paprika, poultry seasoning, onion powder, celery seed, chili powder, sage and thyme in medium bowl. Stir in panko.

2. Place flour in large bowl; slowly whisk in buttermilk and hot pepper sauce until well blended and no longer lumpy.

3. Using fork, dip mushrooms in buttermilk mixture, coating completely and letting excess drip back into bowl. Place in panko; toss to coat. Place on baking sheet.

4. Pour 2 inches of oil into large saucepan or Dutch oven; heat to 360° to 370°F, adjusting heat to maintain temperature during frying. Line large wire rack with paper towels.

5. Working in batches, carefully add mushrooms to hot oil. Cook 2 minutes or until coating is firm and browned. Remove with tongs or slotted spoon; drain on prepared wire rack. Serve with dressing and vegetable sticks.

Oyster mushrooms make a convincing substitute for chicken.

Snacks

BLACK BEAN DIP
MAKES 10 TO 12 SERVINGS

- 1½ tablespoons vegetable oil
- 1 shallot, minced
- 2 cans (about 15 ounces each) black beans, rinsed and drained
- 1 can (4½ ounces) chopped green chiles
- ½ cup cola beverage
- ⅓ cup ketchup
- 1 tablespoon minced chipotle peppers
- 1 teaspoon garlic powder
- 1 teaspoon onion powder
- ¼ to ½ teaspoon ground red pepper
- ½ cup cream cheese, softened
- ½ cup spreadable Cheddar cheese
- ½ cup (2 ounces) shredded sharp Cheddar cheese
- Chopped green onions
- Salsa and sour cream (optional)
- Tortilla chips

1. Preheat oven to 375°F.

2. Heat oil in large saucepan over low heat. Add shallot; cook and stir 5 minutes or until softened. Stir in black beans, chiles, cola beverage, ketchup, chipotle peppers, garlic powder, onion powder and ground red pepper. Bring to a boil over medium-high heat. Reduce heat; simmer 25 minutes or until most liquid is evaporated, stirring frequently. Lightly mash bean mixture with potato masher or fork.

3. Combine cream cheese and spreadable cheese in medium bowl; spread evenly in 8-inch pan. Spoon bean mixture evenly over cheeses and sprinkle with shredded Cheddar cheese.

4. Bake 10 to 15 minutes or until bubbly. Sprinkle with chopped green onions, salsa and sour cream, if desired. Serve with tortilla chips.

Ketchup and cola are unexpected additions to this cheesy bean dip.

Snacks

QUICK AND EASY ARANCINI
MAKES 12 ARANCINI

- 1 package (6 to 8 ounces) sun-dried tomato, mushroom or Milanese risotto mix, plus ingredients to prepare mix*
- ½ cup frozen peas *or* ¼ cup finely chopped oil-packed sun-dried tomatoes (optional)
- ½ cup panko bread crumbs
- ¼ cup finely shredded or grated Parmesan cheese
- 2 tablespoons minced fresh parsley
- 2 tablespoons butter, melted
- 4 ounces Swiss, Asiago or fontina cheese, cut into 12 cubes (about ½ inch)

Or use 3 cups leftover risotto from any risotto recipe.

1. Prepare risotto according to package directions. Stir in peas, if desired. Let stand, uncovered, 20 minutes or until thickened and cool enough to handle.

2. Preheat oven to 375°F. Spray 12 standard (2½-inch) muffin cups with nonstick cooking spray. Combine panko, Parmesan cheese, parsley and melted butter in medium bowl; mix well.

3. Shape level ¼ cupfuls risotto into balls around Swiss cheese cubes, covering completely. Roll in panko mixture to coat. Place in prepared muffin cups.

4. Bake 15 minutes or until arancini are golden brown and cheese cubes are melted. Cool in pan 5 minutes. Serve warm.

Risotto mix is the perfect shortcut for quick and easy arancini.

Snacks

BUFFALO CAULIFLOWER BITES
MAKES 8 SERVINGS

- ¾ cup all-purpose flour
- ¼ cup cornstarch
- 1 teaspoon salt
- ½ teaspoon garlic powder
- ¼ teaspoon black pepper
- 1 cup water
- 1 large head cauliflower (2½ pounds), cut into 1-inch florets
- ½ cup hot pepper sauce
- ¼ cup (½ stick) butter, melted
- Blue cheese or ranch dressing and celery sticks for serving

1. Preheat oven to 450°F. Line baking sheet with foil; spray with nonstick cooking spray.

2. Whisk flour, cornstarch, salt, garlic powder and black pepper in large bowl. Whisk in water until smooth and well blended. Add cauliflower to batter in batches; stir to coat. Arrange on prepared baking sheet.

3. Bake 20 minutes or until cauliflower is lightly browned. Combine hot pepper sauce and butter in small bowl; mix well. Pour over cauliflower; toss until well blended. Bake 5 to 10 minutes or until cauliflower is glazed and crisp, stirring once. Serve with blue cheese or ranch dressing and celery sticks.

You won't even miss the chicken in this spicy snack.

Snacks

CHICKEN IN A BLANKET
MAKES 16 PIECES

- 1 package (11½ ounces) refrigerated breadstick dough (8 count)
- 1 package (10 ounces) Italian-seasoned cooked chicken breast strips
- Ketchup, mustard and/or barbecue sauce

1. Preheat oven to 375°F. Line baking sheet with parchment paper or foil.

2. Unroll dough on cutting board; separate into individual breadsticks. Pat or roll out each piece of dough to 7×1½-inch rectangle (¼ inch thick). Cut each piece of dough in half crosswise to form 16 pieces total.

3. Cut chicken strips in half crosswise. Place one piece of chicken on each piece of dough; wrap dough around chicken and seal, pressing edges together tightly. Place seam side down on prepared baking sheet.

4. Bake 15 to 17 minutes or until light golden brown. Serve warm with mustard and ketchup.

Cooked chicken takes the place of hot dogs in this quick and easy snack.

Snacks

WARM SALSA AND GOAT CHEESE DIP
MAKES ABOUT 8 SERVINGS

- 1¼ cups medium salsa
- 1 log (4 ounces) goat cheese (not crumbles)
- 2 tablespoons coarsely chopped fresh cilantro
- Tortilla chips, pita chips or French bread slices

1. Preheat oven to 350°F.
2. Pour salsa into 9-inch pie plate or shallow 2-quart baking dish. Cut goat cheese crosswise into five pieces; arrange over salsa.
3. Bake about 20 minutes or until salsa is bubbly and cheese is heated through. Sprinkle with cilantro. Serve warm with tortilla chips.

Zesty salsa stands in for homemade tomato sauce in an easy version of this tapas classic.

Snacks

TANGY BARBECUE CHICKEN SKEWERS
MAKES 10 TO 12 SKEWERS

- 1 cup barbecue sauce
- ¼ cup yellow mustard
- 1 pound chicken tenders (about 10 to 12)
- Salt and black pepper

1. Soak 10 to 12 (12-inch) wooden skewers in cold water 20 minutes to prevent burning.

2. Preheat broiler. Combine barbecue sauce and mustard in medium bowl. Weave chicken tenders onto each skewer; season with salt and pepper. Brush each skewer thoroughly with sauce mixture; place on baking sheet or broiler rack. Discard any remaining sauce.

3. Broil skewers 3 minutes. Turn and broil 3 to 5 minutes or until chicken is no longer pink in center.

Mustard spices up easy barbecue chicken snacks.

Snacks

CRUNCHY CHEESE BALL WITH STRAWBERRY-PEPPER SAUCE
MAKES 2 CUPS

- 1 package (3 ounces) ramen noodles, crushed*
- 1 package (8 ounces) cream cheese, softened
- 1 cup (4 ounces) shredded sharp Cheddar cheese
- ¼ cup mayonnaise
- 3 tablespoons finely chopped green onion
- 1 tablespoon Dijon mustard
- ½ teaspoon Worcestershire sauce
- ½ teaspoon curry powder
- ¾ cup chopped pecans, toasted**
- ½ cup strawberry preserves
- 1 jalapeño pepper, seeded and minced
- 1 tablespoon balsamic vinegar
- Assorted crackers
- Apple slices

*Use any flavor; discard seasoning packet.

**To toast pecans, cook in medium skillet over medium heat 3 to 4 minutes or until lightly browned and fragrant, stirring frequently.

1. Combine noodles, cream cheese, Cheddar cheese, mayonnaise, green onion, mustard, Worcestershire sauce and curry powder in food processor; process until well blended. Shape into a ball and wrap in plastic wrap; refrigerate 1 hour. Unwrap cheese ball; roll in pecans to coat evenly. Place on serving plate.

2. Meanwhile, combine preserves, jalapeño and vinegar in small saucepan. Cook over medium heat about 3 minutes or until preserves are dissolved. Remove from heat; refrigerate 30 minutes.

3. Serve cheese ball with crackers, apples and strawberry sauce.

The secrets to a great cheese ball? Add crunch with ramen noodles and a zesty sauce starring strawberry jam.

Snacks

SHORTCUT SPANISH TORTILLA
MAKES 4 TO 6 SERVINGS

- 2 tablespoons olive oil
- 1 medium onion, cut in half and thinly sliced
- 10 eggs
- ½ teaspoon salt
- ⅛ teaspoon black pepper
- 5 ounces potato chips (use plain thin chips, not kettle), lightly crushed
- Chopped fresh chives or parsley (optional)

1. Preheat oven to 350°F. Spray 8-inch round cake pan with nonstick cooking spray.

2. Heat oil in medium skillet over medium-high heat. Add onion; cook and stir 5 minutes or until onion is softened and beginning to brown. Remove from heat; cool 5 minutes.

3. Meanwhile, whisk eggs, salt and pepper in medium bowl until blended. Add potato chips; fold in gently until all chips are coated. Let stand 5 minutes to soften. Stir in onion until well blended. Pour egg mixture into prepared pan; smooth top.

4. Bake 25 minutes or until toothpick inserted into center comes out clean. Cool in pan on wire rack 5 minutes. Loosen tortilla from side of pan, if necessary. Invert tortilla onto plate; invert again onto large serving plate or cutting board. Sprinkle with chives, if desired; serve warm or at room temperature.

Potato chips are the perfect salty, crunchy surprise in this easy, savory snack.

Snacks

SURPRISE CORN MUFFINS
MAKES 12 MUFFINS

- 1 small broccoli crown, broken into florets
- 2 tablespoons water
- 1 cup all-purpose flour
- 1 cup cornmeal
- ¼ cup sugar
- 2 teaspoons baking powder
- 1 teaspoon salt
- 1 cup milk
- 2 eggs
- ¼ cup (½ stick) butter, melted

1. Preheat oven to 400°F. Grease 12 standard (2½-inch) muffin cups or line with paper baking cups. Place broccoli and water in microwavable dish. Cover; cook on HIGH 2 minutes or until crisp-tender.

2. Whisk flour, cornmeal, sugar, baking powder and salt in medium bowl. Whisk milk, eggs and butter in large bowl. Add to flour mixture; stir just until combined.

3. Spoon 1 tablespoon batter into each prepared muffin cup. Place one piece of broccoli in each cup. Add additional batter to each cup, filling about three-fourths full.

4. Bake 15 minutes or until toothpick inserted into centers comes out clean. Cool in pan 5 minutes. Remove to wire rack. Serve warm or cool completely.

The last thing you'd expect in a muffin—a little broccoli tree!

Almond flour makes for delicious low-carb gluten-free meatballs.

Entrées

PESTO TURKEY MEATBALLS
MAKES 4 SERVINGS

- 1 pound ground turkey
- ⅓ cup pesto sauce
- ⅓ cup grated Parmesan cheese, plus additional for garnish
- ¼ cup almond flour
- 1 egg
- 2 green onions, finely chopped
- ½ teaspoon salt, divided
- 2 tablespoons olive oil
- 2 cloves garlic, minced
- ⅛ teaspoon red pepper flakes
- 1 can (28 ounces) whole tomatoes, undrained, crushed with hands or coarsely chopped
- 1 tablespoon tomato paste
- Zucchini noodles, cooked

1. Combine turkey, pesto, ⅓ cup cheese, almond flour, egg, green onions and ¼ teaspoon salt in medium bowl; mix well. Shape mixture into 24 balls (about 1¼ inches). Refrigerate meatballs while preparing sauce.

2. Heat oil in large saucepan or Dutch oven over medium heat. Add garlic and red pepper flakes; cook and stir 2 minutes or until fragrant but not browned. Add tomatoes with liquid, tomato paste and remaining ¼ teaspoon salt; cook 5 minutes or until sauce begins to simmer, stirring occasionally.

3. Remove about 1 cup sauce from saucepan. Arrange meatballs in single layer in saucepan; pour reserved sauce over meatballs. Reduce heat to medium-low; cover and cook 20 minutes.

4. Uncover; increase heat to medium-high. Cook about 10 minutes or until sauce thickens slightly and meatballs are cooked through. Serve over zucchini noodles; garnish with additional cheese.

Entrées

TOFU CAULIFLOWER FRIED RICE
MAKES 4 SERVINGS

- 3 tablespoons soy sauce
- 1 tablespoon plus 1 teaspoon minced fresh ginger, divided
- 2 teaspoons toasted sesame oil
- 1 teaspoon packed brown sugar
- 1 teaspoon rice vinegar
- 1 package (14 ounces) firm tofu, drained and cut into 1-inch cubes
- 2 tablespoons vegetable oil, divided
- 1 yellow or sweet onion, chopped
- 1 carrot, chopped
- ½ cup peas
- 2 cloves garlic, minced
- 1 package (12 ounces) frozen cauliflower rice
- 1 green onion, thinly sliced

1. Whisk soy sauce, 1 tablespoon ginger, sesame oil, brown sugar and vinegar in small bowl. Place tofu in quart-size resealable food storage bag. Pour marinade over tofu. Seal bag, pressing out as much air as possible. Turn to coat tofu with marinade. Refrigerate 3 hours or overnight.

2. Drain tofu, reserving marinade. Heat 1 tablespoon vegetable oil in large skillet over high heat. Add tofu; stir-fry 3 to 5 minutes or until edges are browned. Transfer to bowl.

3. Heat remaining 1 tablespoon vegetable oil in same skillet. Add yellow onion and carrot; stir-fry 2 minutes or until softened. Add peas, garlic and remaining 1 teaspoon ginger; stir-fry 2 minutes or until peas are hot. Add frozen cauliflower rice and ¼ cup reserved marinade; stir-fry 5 minutes or until heated through. Return tofu to skillet; stir-fry until heated through. Top with green onion.

Replace rice with cauliflower for a low-carb veggie-ful twist on fried rice.

Entrées

SKILLET LASAGNA WITH VEGETABLES
MAKES 6 SERVINGS

- 8 ounces Italian turkey or pork sausage, casings removed*
- 8 ounces ground turkey or beef*
- 2 stalks celery, sliced
- ½ cup chopped onion
- 2 cups marinara sauce
- 1⅓ cups water
- 4 ounces uncooked bowtie (farfalle) pasta
- 1 medium zucchini, halved lengthwise, then cut crosswise into ½-inch slices (2 cups)
- ¾ cup chopped green or yellow bell pepper
- ½ cup (2 ounces) shredded mozzarella cheese
- ½ cup ricotta cheese
- 2 tablespoons finely grated Parmesan cheese

Or substitute 1 pound of ground beef or 1 pound of Italian sauce for the combination.

1. Heat large skillet over medium-high heat. Add sausage, ground turkey, celery and onion; cook and stir 6 to 8 minutes or until turkey is no longer pink, stirring to break up meat. Stir in marinara sauce and water; bring to a boil. Stir in pasta. Reduce heat to medium-low; cover and simmer 12 minutes.

2. Stir in zucchini and bell pepper; cover and simmer 2 minutes. Uncover and simmer 4 to 6 minutes or until vegetables are crisp-tender.

3. Sprinkle with mozzarella cheese. Combine ricotta and Parmesan cheeses in small bowl; stir to blend. Drop by rounded teaspoonfuls on top of mixture in skillet. Remove from heat; cover and let stand 10 minutes.

Bowtie pasta is a fun substitute for lasagna noodles in this quick skillet dinner.

Entrées

BISCUIT-TOPPED CHICKEN POT PIE
MAKES 6 SERVINGS

- 1½ pounds boneless skinless chicken breasts, cut into 1-inch pieces
- ¼ cup chicken broth
- 1 package (16 ounces) frozen mixed vegetables, such as cauliflower, carrots, broccoli, zucchini and red bell pepper
- 1 can (10¾ ounces) condensed cream of chicken soup, undiluted
- 4 tablespoons grated Parmesan cheese, divided
- 1 teaspoon dried thyme
- ½ teaspoon black pepper
- 1½ cups biscuit baking mix
- ½ cup milk

1. Preheat oven to 400°F. Combine chicken and broth in large saucepan; bring to a boil over high heat. Reduce heat; simmer 8 minutes or until chicken is cooked through, stirring occasionally.

2. Stir in vegetables, soup, 2 tablespoons cheese, thyme and pepper; mix well. Cook until heated through. Transfer mixture to 8-inch square baking dish.

3. Combine baking mix and milk in small bowl; mix just until dry ingredients are moistened. Drop batter by heaping tablespoonfuls over hot chicken mixture; sprinkle with remaining 2 tablespoons cheese.

4. Bake 14 to 16 minutes or until bubbly and biscuits are golden brown.

Tip

Freeze leftovers in smaller baking dishes for another day. To reheat a frozen casserole, unwrap it and microwave, covered, at HIGH 20 to 30 minutes, stirring once or twice during cooking. Allow to stand 5 minutes before serving.

Simplify your pot pie with canned soup and biscuit baking mix.

Entrées

VEGGIE "MEATBALLS"
MAKES 4 SERVINGS

- ½ cup water
- ¾ cup bulgur wheat
- 2 teaspoons olive oil
- 3 medium portobello mushrooms (10 ounces), stemmed and diced
- 1 small onion, chopped
- 1 small zucchini, grated and squeezed dry
- 1 teaspoon Italian seasoning
- 2 cloves garlic, minced
- ¼ cup sun-dried tomatoes (not packed in oil*), chopped
- 4 ounces grated Parmesan cheese
- Salt and black pepper
- 2 egg whites
- 2 cups marinara sauce, heated

*If unavailable you may substitute ¼ cup sun-dried tomatoes packed in oil, well drained, patted dry and chopped.

1. Preheat oven to 375°F. Line large baking sheet with foil; spray with nonstick cooking spray.

2. Bring water to a boil in small saucepan; remove from heat. Stir in bulgur; cover and let stand while preparing vegetables.

3. Heat oil in large nonstick skillet over medium-high heat. Add mushrooms, onion, zucchini and Italian seasoning; cook and stir about 8 minutes or until softened. Add garlic; cook and stir 1 minute. Stir in tomatoes.

4. Transfer mushroom mixture to large bowl; let cool slightly. Add bulgur and cheese; taste and season with salt and pepper. Stir in egg whites; mix well. Shape mixture by ¼ cupfuls into 12 balls for each. Place meatballs on prepared baking sheet.

5. Bake 20 minutes. Turn meatballs; bake 8 to 10 minutes or until well browned. Serve hot with marinara sauce.

No meat here! Veggies and bulgur take the place of ground beef.

Entrées

JALAPEÑO-LIME CHICKEN
MAKES 8 SERVINGS

- 8 bone-in chicken thighs
- 3 tablespoons jalapeño jelly
- 1 tablespoon olive oil
- 1 tablespoon lime juice
- 1 clove garlic, minced
- 1 teaspoon chili powder
- ½ teaspoon salt
- ½ teaspoon black pepper

1. Preheat oven to 400°F. Line 15×10-inch baking sheet with parchment paper or foil; spray with nonstick cooking spray.

2. Arrange chicken in single layer in prepared pan. Bake 15 minutes; drain off juices.

3. Meanwhile, combine jelly, oil, lime juice, garlic, chili powder, salt and pepper in small bowl. Turn chicken; brush with half of jelly mixture.

4. Bake 20 minutes. Turn chicken; brush with remaining jelly mixture. Bake chicken 10 to 15 minutes or until cooked through (165°F).

Jalapeño jelly is the sweet and spicy secret to this tasty chicken.

Entrées

TURKEY MEAT LOAF
MAKES 8 SERVINGS

- 2 pounds ground turkey
- 1 cup grated zucchini, squeezed dry
- ¾ cup diced red bell pepper
- ¾ cup diced green bell pepper
- ½ cup old-fashioned oats
- 2 eggs, beaten
- 1 tablespoon ketchup
- 1 teaspoon salt
- 1 teaspoon dried thyme
- 1 teaspoon Dijon mustard
- ½ teaspoon black pepper
- Chopped fresh parsley (optional)

1. Preheat oven to 400°F. Spray 9×5-inch loaf pan with nonstick cooking spray. Line bottom with waxed paper or parchment paper. Spray paper with cooking spray.

2. Combine turkey, zucchini, bell peppers, oats, eggs, ketchup, salt, thyme, mustard and black pepper in large bowl; mix well. Place in prepared pan, pressing down with spoon or spatula to pack firmly and level top.

3. Bake 1 hour or until cooked through (165°F). Cool on wire rack 15 minutes.

4. Run spatula around edges to loosen. Place 10-inch plate on top of pan; invert meat loaf onto plate. Remove waxed paper or parchment from bottom. Turn right side up; sprinkle with parsley, if desired.

Zucchini adds moisture and fiber to level up your meat loaf.

Entrées

SQUASH LASAGNA
MAKES 8 SERVINGS

- 1 medium eggplant
- 2 medium zucchini
- 2 medium yellow squash
- 1¼ pounds Italian turkey or pork sausage, casings removed
- 2 medium bell peppers, diced
- 2 cups mushrooms, thinly sliced
- 1 can (about 14 ounces) diced tomatoes
- 1 cup tomato sauce
- ½ cup coarsely chopped fresh basil
- 1 teaspoon dried oregano
- ½ teaspoon salt
- ¼ teaspoon black pepper
- 1 container (15 ounces) ricotta cheese
- 2 cups (8 ounces) shredded mozzarella cheese
- ¼ cup grated Parmesan cheese

1. Cut eggplant, zucchini and yellow squash lengthwise into thin (⅛- to ¼-inch) slices. To reduce excess water, place slices in colander and drain 1 to 2 hours (see Tip).

2. Preheat oven to 375°F. Heat large nonstick skillet over medium-high heat. Add sausage; cook 8 to 10 minutes or until cooked through, stirring to break up meat. Drain fat. Transfer to plate.

3. Add bell peppers and mushrooms to skillet; cook and stir 3 to 4 minutes or until vegetables are tender. Return sausage to skillet. Add tomatoes, tomato sauce, basil, oregano, salt and black pepper; cook and stir 1 to 2 minutes or until heated through.

4. Layer one third of eggplant, zucchini and yellow squash in 13×9-inch nonstick baking pan. Spread half of ricotta cheese over vegetables. Top with one third of tomato sauce mixture. Sprinkle evenly with half of mozzarella cheese. Repeat layers once, ending with final layer of vegetables and tomato sauce mixture. Sprinkle with Parmesan cheese; cover with foil.

5. Bake 45 minutes. Remove foil; bake 10 to 15 minutes or until vegetables are tender. Let stand 10 minutes before cutting.

Tip

To reduce excess water from eggplant and squash, place in a colander. Lay a paper towel or clean kitchen towel over the vegetables and weigh them down with a heavy bowl. Let vegetables drain for 1 to 2 hours before preparing recipe. Or bake vegetables 10 minutes in a preheated 350°F oven.

Eggplant, zucchini and summer squash stand in for pasta in this version of lasagna.

Entrées

HOT SWEET MUSTARD CHICKEN
MAKES 4 TO 6 SERVINGS

4 cups small pretzel twists

8 boneless skinless chicken thighs* (about 2 pounds)

Salt and black pepper

½ cup hot sweet mustard

Boneless skinless chicken breasts can also be used; reduce cooking time to 20 to 25 minutes.

1. Preheat oven to 350°F. Line baking sheet with foil; place wire rack over foil and spray with nonstick cooking spray.

2. Place pretzels in large resealable food storage bag; seal bag. Crush pretzels with rolling pin, meat mallet or heavy skillet. (Pretzels should yield about 2 cups crumbs.) Place pretzel crumbs in shallow dish.

3. Season chicken with salt and pepper. Generously brush all sides of chicken with mustard; coat with pretzel crumbs, pressing crumbs into mustard to adhere. Place chicken on prepared rack.

4. Bake 35 to 40 minutes or until chicken is cooked through (175°F).

Instead of bread crumbs, coat chicken with pretzels!

Entrées

BALSAMIC CHICKEN
MAKES 4 SERVINGS

- 2 tablespoons olive oil, divided
- ½ cup chopped shallots
- 1 cup cola beverage
- ⅓ cup balsamic vinegar
- 2 tablespoons chopped fresh basil
- 2 cloves garlic, minced
- ½ teaspoon salt
- ½ teaspoon black pepper
- 1½ pounds boneless skinless chicken cutlets

1. Prepare grill for direct cooking over medium-high heat. Oil grid.

2. Heat 1 tablespoon oil in large nonstick skillet over medium heat. Add shallots; cook and stir 3 minutes or until tender. Add cola and vinegar; reduce heat to low. Simmer 10 minutes or until reduced to ⅔ cup. Reserve ¼ cup sauce in small bowl; set aside.

3. Combine basil, garlic, salt and pepper in small bowl. Place chicken on baking sheet; pat garlic mixture evenly over chicken. Drizzle with remaining 1 tablespoon oil.

4. Grill chicken 3 minutes per side or until cooked through (165°F), basting with reserved ¼ cup sauce. Serve immediately with remaining sauce.

Cola makes a sweet and tangy glaze for chicken.

Entrées

SWEET STICKY PINEAPPLE CHICKEN WITH RICE
MAKES 4 SERVINGS

- 2 tablespoons vegetable oil
- 1 onion, chopped
- 2 teaspoons minced garlic
- 1 teaspoon ground ginger
- 1 teaspoon five-spice powder
- 1 can (12 ounces) cola beverage
- 1 cup ketchup
- 1 can (20 ounces) pineapple chunks in juice, drained
- ¼ cup packed brown sugar
- ¼ cup soy sauce
- 2 tablespoons white vinegar
- 4 boneless skinless chicken breasts (about 6 ounces each)
- 2 cups uncooked rice
- 1 can (8 ounces) crushed pineapple, drained
- 1 tablespoon chopped fresh parsley

1. Preheat oven to 350°F. Spray 13×9-inch baking dish with nonstick cooking spray.

2. Heat oil in medium saucepan over medium heat. Add onion; cook and stir 8 minutes or until soft and translucent. Stir in garlic, ginger and five-spice powder; cook 1 minute. Add cola, ketchup, pineapple chunks, brown sugar, soy sauce and vinegar; bring to a boil over medium-high heat until mixture is slightly syrupy, about 15 minutes.

3. Place chicken in prepared baking dish; top with pineapple mixture. Bake 30 minutes, turning every 10 minutes. Remove to cutting board; let stand 5 minutes.

4. Meanwhile, cook rice according to package directions. Stir in crushed pineapple and parsley. Divide rice among four serving plates; top with chicken, pineapple and sauce.

Cola and double pineapple make a delicious tropical-inspired meal.

Entrées

CHEESE RAVIOLI WITH PUMPKIN SAUCE
MAKES 6 SERVINGS

- 1 tablespoon olive oil
- ⅓ cup sliced green onions
- 2 cloves garlic, minced
- ½ teaspoon whole fennel seeds
- 1 cup evaporated milk
- 1 tablespoon all-purpose flour
- ¼ teaspoon salt
- ⅛ teaspoon black pepper
- ½ cup canned pumpkin
- 2 packages (9 ounces each) uncooked refrigerated cheese ravioli
- 2 tablespoons grated Parmesan cheese

1. Heat oil in medium saucepan over medium heat. Add green onions, garlic and fennel seeds; cook and stir 3 minutes or until green onions are tender.

2. Whisk evaporated milk, flour, salt and pepper in small bowl until smooth; stir into saucepan. Bring to a boil over high heat; boil until thickened, stirring constantly. Stir in pumpkin; reduce heat to low.

3. Meanwhile, cook ravioli according to package directions; drain. Divide ravioli evenly among six plates. Top with pumpkin sauce; sprinkle with cheese. Serve immediately.

Ravioli doesn't need classic marinara sauce when it has autumn-inspired pumpkin sauce.

Simple aglio e olio gets a twisty makeover with the addition of vibrant beets.

Pasta

SPAGHETTI AND BEETS AGLIO E OLIO
MAKES 6 SERVINGS

- 8 ounces uncooked spaghetti or thin spaghetti
- 2 medium beets, peeled
- ⅓ cup plus 2 tablespoons olive oil, divided
- 1 cup fresh Italian or French bread crumbs*
- 4 cloves garlic, very thinly sliced
- ¾ teaspoon salt
- ½ teaspoon red pepper flakes
- ½ cup chopped fresh Italian parsley
- ¾ cup shredded Parmesan cheese, divided

*To make fresh bread crumbs, tear 2 ounces bread into pieces; process in food processor until coarse crumbs form.

1. Cook pasta in large saucepan of salted boiling water according to package directions for al dente. Drain and return to saucepan, reserving ½ cup water; keep warm.

2. Meanwhile, spiral beets with fine spiral blade; cut into desired lengths. Heat 1 tablespoon oil in large skillet over medium-high heat. Add beets; cook and stir 8 to 10 minutes or until tender.

3. Heat 1 tablespoon oil in large skillet over medium heat. Add bread crumbs; cook 4 to 5 minutes or until golden brown, stirring frequently. Transfer to small bowl.

4. Add remaining ⅓ cup oil, garlic, salt and red pepper flakes to same skillet; cook about 3 minutes or until garlic just begins to brown on edges.

5. Add pasta, beets and parsley to skillet; toss to coat with oil mixture. Add some of reserved pasta water to moisten pasta, if desired. Stir in bread crumbs and ½ cup cheese. Top with remaining ¼ cup cheese just before serving.

Pasta

LENTIL RAGÙ
MAKES 6 TO 8 SERVINGS

- 2 tablespoons olive oil
- 1 onion, chopped
- 1 carrot, chopped
- 1 stalk celery, chopped
- 2 cloves garlic, minced
- 1 teaspoon salt
- ½ teaspoon dried oregano
- Pinch red pepper flakes
- 3 tablespoons tomato paste
- ¼ cup dry white wine
- 1 can (28 ounces) crushed tomatoes
- 1 can (about 14 ounces) diced tomatoes
- 1 cup dried lentils,* rinsed
- 1 portobello mushroom, gills removed, finely chopped
- 1½ cups water or vegetable broth
- Hot cooked pasta

*Packages of dried lentils occasionally contain grit or tiny stones. Sort through and discard any foreign matter.

1. Heat oil in large saucepan over medium heat. Add onion, carrot and celery; cook and stir 10 minutes or until onion is lightly browned and carrot is softened.

2. Stir in garlic, salt, oregano and red pepper flakes. Add tomato paste; cook and stir 1 minute. Add wine; cook and stir until absorbed. Stir in crushed tomatoes, diced tomatoes, lentils, mushroom and water; bring to a simmer.

3. Reduce heat to low; partially cover and simmer about 40 minutes or until lentils are tender, removing cover after 20 minutes. Serve over pasta.

Hearty meat sauce gets a vegan makeover with lentils instead of ground beef or pork.

Pasta

SAUSAGE SPAGHETTI
MAKES 4 SERVINGS

- 1 package (about 14 ounces) smoked sausage
- 8 ounces uncooked thick spaghetti or regular spaghetti
- ¼ cup olive oil or butter
- 2 cloves garlic, minced
- ¼ cup grated Parmesan cheese
- Salt, black pepper and red pepper flakes

1. Cut sausage into ¼-inch slices. Stick 5 spaghetti noodles into each slice.

2. Bring large saucepan of salted water to a boil. Add pasta and sausage; push fully into water as noodles soften. Cook 9 to 10 minutes or until pasta is tender, stirring frequently to prevent sticking; drain.

3. Heat oil in large saucepan over medium heat. Add garlic; cook 30 seconds. Add pasta and sausage; toss to coat. Remove from heat; top with cheese. Season with salt, black pepper and red pepper flakes.

Variations

For cheesy sausage spaghetti, melt 2 tablespoons butter in medium saucepan over medium-high heat. Whisk in 2 tablespoons flour until smooth and well blended; cook 1 minute without browning. Gradually whisk in 1½ cups milk; cook until thickened, stirring frequently. Whisk in 8 ounces shredded cheese (American, Cheddar, Monterey Jack, Swiss or a combination) until melted and smooth. Season with salt. Pour sauce over pasta; stir to coat.

For Italian sausage spaghetti, use smoked Italian sausage instead of regular smoked sausage and top with warm marinara sauce.

Smoked sausage is a savory secret in a simple spaghetti dinner.

Pasta

TOMATO AND BRIE NOODLES
MAKES 6 SERVINGS

- 1 pint grape tomatoes, halved
- 2 teaspoons olive oil
- ¾ teaspoon salt, divided
- 4 cups uncooked egg noodles
- 2 tablespoons butter
- 1 clove garlic, smashed
- 2 tablespoons all-purpose flour
- 2 cups half-and-half
- 8 ounces good-quality ripe Brie, crust removed, cut into small chunks
- ¼ cup finely chopped fresh basil
- 2 tablespoons minced fresh chives
- ¼ teaspoon pepper
- ¼ cup sliced almonds

1. Preheat oven to 425°F. Line large baking sheet with foil. Spray 9-inch square baking dish with nonstick cooking spray.

2. Spread tomatoes on prepared baking sheet; drizzle with oil and sprinkle with ¼ teaspoon salt. Roast 20 minutes or until tomatoes are tender and slightly shriveled. Set aside. *Reduce oven temperature to 350°F.*

3. Meanwhile, cook noodles in large saucepan of salted boiling water according to package directions for al dente. Drain and return to saucepan; keep warm.

4. Melt butter in large saucepan or deep skillet over medium heat. Add garlic clove and cook 1 minute. Stir in flour until blended. Gradually add half-and-half; cook and stir until thickened. Remove and discard garlic. Gradually stir in cheese until melted.

5. Add basil, chives, remaining ½ teaspoon salt and pepper. Stir in noodles. Drain off any liquid from tomatoes; fold into noodle mixture. Spread in prepared baking dish.

6. Bake 17 to 20 minutes or until sauce starts to bubble. Sprinkle with almonds; bake 8 to 10 minutes or until nuts are light golden brown.

Brie is an unexpected cheese to use in a grown-up version of macaroni and cheese.

Pasta

PASTA PRIMAVERA WITH RICOTTA
MAKES 4 SERVINGS

- 8 ounces uncooked fettuccine
- 1 cup ricotta cheese
- ½ cup milk
- 1 zucchini
- 1 yellow squash
- 1 red bell pepper
- 1 tablespoon olive oil
- 1 clove garlic, minced
- ½ teaspoon red pepper flakes
- 1 cup peas
- 1 teaspoon Italian seasoning
- ½ teaspoon salt
- ½ cup grated Parmesan cheese

1. Cook fettuccine in large saucepan of salted boiling water according to package directions for al dente. Drain and return to saucepan; keep warm. Whisk ricotta cheese and milk in small bowl.

2. Meanwhile, spiral zucchini and yellow squash with fine spiral blade of spiralizer and spiral bell pepper with spiral slicing blade. Cut vegetables to desired lengths.

3. Heat oil in large nonstick skillet over medium heat. Add garlic and red pepper flakes; cook and stir 1 minute. Add zucchini, yellow squash, bell pepper, peas, Italian seasoning and salt; cook and stir 5 minutes or until vegetables are crisp-tender.

4. Combine fettuccine, vegetables and ricotta cheese mixture in large bowl; mix gently until well blended. Sprinkle with Parmesan cheese just before serving.

Tip

If you don't have a spiralizer, substitute a package of mixed spiralized zucchini and summer squash from the produce section of the grocery store and thinly slice the bell pepper with a knife.

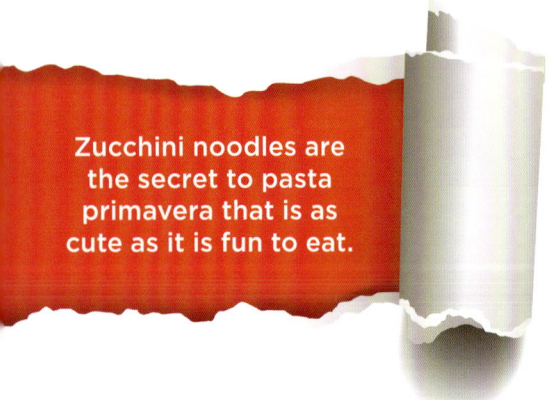

Zucchini noodles are the secret to pasta primavera that is as cute as it is fun to eat.

Pasta

PUMPKIN MAC AND CHEESE
MAKES 6 TO 8 SERVINGS

- 1 package (16 ounces) uncooked large elbow macaroni or medium shell pasta
- ½ cup (1 stick) butter, divided
- ¼ cup all-purpose flour
- 1½ cups milk
- 1 teaspoon salt, divided
- ¼ teaspoon ground nutmeg
- ⅛ teaspoon ground red pepper
- 2 cups (8 ounces) shredded Cheddar cheese
- 1 cup (4 ounces) shredded Monterey Jack cheese
- 1 cup canned pumpkin
- 1 cup panko bread crumbs
- ½ cup chopped hazelnuts or walnuts (optional)
- ⅛ teaspoon dried sage
- 1 cup (4 ounces) shredded Chihuahua cheese*

If Chihuahua cheese is not available, substitute Monterey Jack cheese.

1. Preheat oven to 350°F. Spray 2-quart baking dish with nonstick cooking spray. Cook macaroni in large saucepan of salted boiling water according to package directions for al dente. Drain and return to saucepan; keep warm.

2. Melt ¼ cup butter in medium saucepan over medium-high heat. Whisk in flour until smooth; cook 1 minute without browning, whisking constantly. Gradually whisk in milk in thin steady stream. Add ¾ teaspoon salt, nutmeg and red pepper; cook 2 to 3 minutes or until thickened, stirring frequently. Gradually add Cheddar and Monterey Jack cheeses, stirring after each addition until smooth. Add pumpkin; cook 1 minute or until heated through, stirring constantly. Pour sauce over pasta; stir to coat.

3. For topping, melt remaining ¼ cup butter in small skillet over medium-low heat; cook until golden brown. Remove from heat; stir in panko, hazelnuts, if desired, sage and remaining ¼ teaspoon salt.

4. Spread half of pasta in prepared baking dish; sprinkle with ½ cup Chihuahua cheese. Top with remaining pasta; sprinkle with remaining Chihuahua cheese. Top with panko mixture.

5. Bake 25 to 30 minutes or until topping is golden brown and pasta is heated through.

Pumpkin is the secret to extra creamy mac and cheese with less cheese.

Pasta

MOCK FRIED RICE
MAKES 4 SERVINGS

- 1 package (3 ounces) ramen noodles*
- 1 tablespoon vegetable oil
- 1½ cups small broccoli florets
- ½ cup chopped red bell pepper
- ½ cup shredded carrot
- 1 green onion, chopped
- 2 tablespoons soy sauce
- 1 egg, beaten

*Use any flavor; discard seasoning packet.

1. Cook noodles according to package directions. Drain and let cool to room temperature. Refrigerate until cold. Coarsely chop noodles or cut into 3-inch lengths with kitchen scissors.

2. Heat oil in wok or large nonstick skillet over medium-high heat. Add broccoli, bell pepper, carrot and green onion; stir-fry 3 minutes or until crisp-tender.

3. Add noodles and soy sauce to wok. Push mixture up side of wok or to one side of skillet; add egg. Cook until egg is set, stirring constantly and breaking into pieces with wooden spoon. Stir egg into noodles until well blended. Serve immediately.

Variation

For a heartier dish, stir in 8 ounces of cubed tofu or cooked chicken or shrimp with the broccoli.

The secret to quick and easy fried rice is actually noodles!

Pasta

CAULIFLOWER MAC AND GOUDA
MAKES 4 TO 6 SERVINGS

- 1 package (16 ounces) uncooked bowtie (farfalle) pasta
- 4 cups milk
- 2 cloves garlic, smashed
- ¼ cup (½ stick) plus 3 tablespoons butter, divided
- 5 tablespoons all-purpose flour
- 1 teaspoon dry mustard
- ⅛ teaspoon smoked paprika or regular paprika
- 1 pound Gouda cheese, shredded
- Salt and black pepper
- 1 head cauliflower, cored and cut into florets
- 1 cup panko bread crumbs

1. Cook pasta according to package directions in large saucepan of boiling salted water until al dente. Scoop out pasta with large slotted spoon; place in large bowl and keep warm. Reserve pasta water in saucepan; return water to a boil.

2. Meanwhile, bring milk and garlic to a boil in medium saucepan. Reduce heat; keep warm. Discard garlic.

3. Melt ¼ cup butter in medium saucepan over medium-high heat. Whisk in flour until smooth; cook 1 minute without browning, whisking constantly. Gradually whisk in milk in thin steady stream. Cook 2 to 3 minutes or until thickened, stirring frequently.

4. Stir in mustard and paprika. Add cheese by handfuls, stirring until well blended and melted after each addition. Season with salt and pepper. Keep warm.

5. Preheat broiler. Add cauliflower to boiling pasta water. Cook 3 to 5 minutes or just until tender; drain. Add cauliflower and sauce mixture to pasta; mix well. Spoon pasta mixture into 4 to 6 individual baking dishes or 13×9-inch baking dish.

6. Melt remaining 3 tablespoons butter in small saucepan over medium heat; stir in panko. Remove from heat. Sprinkle panko mixture over pasta mixture. Broil 2 minutes or until golden brown.

Bowtie pasta is the "secret" ingredient in a classic cauliflower and cheese sauce side dish.

Pasta

LINGUINE WITH SUN-DRIED TOMATO PESTO
MAKES 4 SERVINGS

- 8 ounces uncooked linguine or spaghetti
- ½ cup sun-dried tomatoes (not packed in oil)
- ½ cup packed fresh basil leaves
- 2 tablespoons olive oil
- 2 tablespoons grated Parmesan cheese, plus additional for serving
- 1 teaspoon dried oregano
- 1 clove garlic
- Salt and black pepper

1. Cook linguine in large saucepan of salted boiling water according to package directions for al dente. Drain and return to saucepan; keep warm.

2. Meanwhile, combine sun-dried tomatoes and ½ cup hot water in small bowl; soak 3 to 5 minutes or until tomatoes are soft and pliable. Drain; reserve liquid.

3. Combine tomatoes, basil, oil, 2 tablespoons cheese, oregano and garlic in food processor or blender. Process until mixture is a medium thick sauce consistency, adding reserved tomato water as necessary. Season with salt and pepper. Spoon over pasta; toss to coat. Serve immediately with additional cheese.

Twist up your pesto game by adding sweet and tangy sun-dried tomatoes.

Pasta

RAMEN ALFREDO
MAKES 2 SERVINGS

- 1 cup whipping cream
- ¼ teaspoon salt
- ¼ teaspoon black pepper
- ⅛ teaspoon ground nutmeg
- 3 packages (3 ounces each) ramen noodles*
- ½ cup grated Parmesan cheese, plus additional for garnish
- Chopped fresh parsley (optional)

Use any flavor; discard seasoning packets.

1. Combine cream, salt, pepper and nutmeg in large saucepan; cook over medium heat 8 minutes or until reduced to ½ cup, stirring occasionally.

2. Bring large saucepan of salted water to a boil. Add noodles; cook 1 minute, stirring with fork to break up noodles. Drain noodles, reserving ¼ cup cooking water.

3. Add reserved cooking water and ½ cup cheese to cream mixture; bring to a simmer over medium-high heat. Reduce heat to medium-low; add noodles, tossing to coat. Cook 1 minute or until noodles are al dente and cheese is melted. Sprinkle with additional cheese and parsley, if desired.

Ramen noodles make this simple classic dish extra fun (and extra easy with a 1-minute cook time).

Pepperoni turns this healthy whole grain side into forkfuls of pizza.

Sides & Casseroles

FARRO, MOZZARELLA AND PEPPERONI SALAD
MAKES 6 TO 8 SERVINGS

- 1 cup uncooked pearled farro, rinsed
- 1 can (14 ounces) quartered artichoke hearts, drained
- 1 package (8 ounces) fresh mozzarella pearls (small balls)
- 1 red bell pepper, chopped
- ½ cup chopped red onion
- ½ cup chopped fresh basil
- 1 ounce (17 slices) turkey pepperoni, halved
- ¼ cup canola oil
- 3 tablespoons red wine vinegar
- ½ teaspoon salt
- ½ teaspoon black pepper

1. Cook farro according to package directions.
2. Meanwhile, combine artichokes, cheese, bell pepper, onion, basil, pepperoni, oil, vinegar, salt and black pepper in large bowl; mix well.
3. Drain farro in fine-mesh strainer; rinse under cold water to cool quickly. Drain well.
4. Add farro to salad; toss gently to coat.

Sides & Casseroles

PUMPKIN RISOTTO
MAKES 4 SERVINGS

- 4 cups vegetable broth
- 5 whole fresh sage leaves
- ¼ teaspoon ground nutmeg
- 2 tablespoons butter
- 1 tablespoon olive oil
- 1 onion, finely chopped
- 2 cloves garlic, minced
- 1½ cups uncooked arborio rice
- ½ cup dry white wine
- 1 teaspoon salt
- Black pepper
- 1 can (15 ounces) pumpkin purée
- ½ cup shredded Parmesan cheese
- 2 tablespoons chopped fresh sage, divided
- ¼ cup toasted pepitas (pumpkin seeds) or chopped toasted walnuts or pecans

1. Combine broth, whole sage leaves and nutmeg in small saucepan; bring to a boil over high heat. Reduce heat to low to maintain a simmer.

2. Heat butter and oil in large saucepan over medium-high heat. Add onion; cook and stir 5 minutes or until softened. Add garlic; cook and stir 30 seconds. Add rice; cook 2 to 3 minutes or until rice appears translucent, stirring frequently to coat with butter. Add wine and salt; cook until most of liquid is absorbed. Season with pepper.

3. Add broth mixture, ½ cup at a time, stirring frequently until broth is absorbed before adding next ½ cup (discard whole sage leaves). Stir in pumpkin when about 1 cup broth remains. Add remaining broth; cook until rice is al dente, stirring constantly. (Total cook time will be about 25 minutes.)

4. Remove from heat; stir in cheese and 1 tablespoon chopped sage. Cover and let stand 5 minutes. Top each serving with 1 tablespoon pumpkin seeds and remaining chopped sage.

Pumpkin adds a ton of creaminess to a classic risotto.

Sides & Casseroles

RAMEN TAMALE PIE
MAKES 6 SERVINGS

- 2 teaspoons vegetable oil
- ½ medium onion, diced
- 1 jalapeño pepper, minced
- 1 pound ground beef
- 1 can (about 14 ounces) fire-roasted diced tomatoes
- 1 package (3 ounces) beef-flavored ramen noodles, crumbled
- 1 teaspoon ground cumin
- 1 cup frozen corn
- 1 package (8½ ounces) corn muffin mix
- ⅓ cup milk
- 1 egg, beaten
- ½ cup (2 ounces) shredded Cheddar cheese

1. Preheat oven to 400°F.

2. Heat oil in large skillet over medium heat. Add onion and jalapeño; cook and stir 5 minutes or until softened. Add beef; cook 6 to 8 minutes or until browned, stirring to break up meat. Drain fat. Add tomatoes, ramen seasoning packet and cumin; mix well. Remove from heat; stir in corn and half of noodles. Pour mixture into 9-inch baking dish.

3. Combine muffin mix, milk and egg in large bowl; mix well. Spread over beef mixture; sprinkle with cheese and remaining noodles.

4. Bake 30 to 35 minutes or until corn bread is golden brown and filling is heated through.

Ramen noodles work as both a filling and crunchy topping.

Sides & Casseroles

CAULIFLOWER PICNIC SALAD
MAKES 6 SERVINGS

- 1 teaspoon salt
- 1 head cauliflower, cut into 1-inch florets
- ¾ cup mayonnaise
- 1 tablespoon yellow mustard
- 2 tablespoons minced fresh parsley
- ⅓ cup chopped dill pickle
- ⅓ cup minced red onion
- 2 hard-cooked eggs, peeled and chopped
- Salt and black pepper

1. Fill large saucepan with 1 inch water. Bring to a simmer over medium-high heat; stir in salt. Add cauliflower; reduce heat to medium. Cover and cook 5 to 7 minutes or until cauliflower is fork-tender but not mushy. Drain and cool slightly.

2. Whisk mayonnaise, mustard and parsley in large bowl. Stir in pickle and onion. Gently fold in cauliflower and eggs. Season to taste with salt and pepper.

Replace potatoes with cauliflower for a healthier version of classic potato salad.

Sides & Casseroles

JALAPEÑO BEANS
MAKES 4 TO 6 SERVINGS

- 1 tablespoon vegetable oil
- 1 small onion, finely chopped
- 1 teaspoon ground cumin
- 1 teaspoon garlic powder
- ½ teaspoon smoked paprika
- ¼ teaspoon ground red pepper
- 3 tablespoons chopped pickled jalapeño peppers
- 2 cans (about 15 ounces each) chili beans (made with pinto beans)
- ⅓ cup dark lager beer
- 1 tablespoon white vinegar
- 1 teaspoon sugar
- ½ teaspoon hot pepper sauce
- Salt and black pepper

1. Heat oil in large saucepan over medium-high heat. Add onion; cook and stir 2 minutes or until translucent. Add cumin, garlic powder, smoked paprika and red pepper; cook and stir 1 minute. Add pickled jalapeños; cook and stir 30 seconds.

2. Stir in beans, beer, vinegar, sugar and hot pepper sauce; bring to a boil. Reduce heat to medium-low; cook 15 minutes, stirring occasionally. Season with salt and black pepper. Beans will thicken upon standing.

Dark beer gives these zesty beans a little something extra.

Sides & Casseroles

BACON BROCCOLI SLAW
MAKES 6 TO 8 SERVINGS

- 1 package (12 ounces) broccoli slaw
- 6 slices bacon, crisp-cooked and crumbled
- ½ small red onion, chopped
- 1 package (3 ounces) ramen noodles, crumbled, divided*
- ¼ cup roasted salted sunflower seeds
- 1 cup mayonnaise
- 2 tablespoons sugar
- 2 tablespoons cider vinegar
- ¼ teaspoon black pepper

*Use any flavor; discard seasoning packet.

1. Combine broccoli slaw, bacon, onion, half of noodles and sunflower seeds in large bowl.
2. Whisk mayonnaise, sugar, vinegar and pepper in small bowl. Pour over slaw mixture; stir to combine. Garnish with remaining noodles. Serve immediately.

Tip

Any chopped nuts, such as peanuts or almonds, can be substituted for the sunflower seeds.

Make crunchy broccoli slaw even crunchier by stirring in ramen noodles.

Sides & Casseroles

FRUITED CORN PUDDING
MAKES 8 SERVINGS

- 5 cups thawed frozen corn, divided
- 5 eggs
- ½ cup milk
- 1½ cups whipping cream
- ⅓ cup butter, melted and cooled
- 1 teaspoon vanilla
- ½ teaspoon salt
- ¼ teaspoon ground nutmeg
- 3 tablespoons finely chopped dried apricots
- 3 tablespoons dried cranberries or raisins
- 3 tablespoons finely chopped dates
- 2 tablespoons finely chopped dried pears or other dried fruit

1. Preheat oven to 350°F. Grease 13×9-inch baking dish.
2. Combine 3½ cups corn, eggs and milk in food processor; process until almost smooth.
3. Transfer corn mixture to large bowl. Add cream, butter, vanilla, salt and nutmeg; stir until well blended. Add remaining 1½ cups corn, apricots, cranberries, dates and pears; mix well. Pour into prepared baking dish.
4. Bake 50 to 60 minutes or until center is set and top begins to brown. Let stand 10 to 15 minutes before serving.

Tart fruit is an unexpected surprise in this decadent, creamy corn pudding.

Sides & Casseroles

GRILLED ROMAINE WITH TANGY VINAIGRETTE
MAKES 6 SERVINGS

TANGY VINAIGRETTE
- 3 cups cola beverage
- ⅓ cup white vinegar
- ⅓ cup canola oil
- ¼ cup sugar
- 3 tablespoons ketchup
- 2 tablespoons honey mustard
- 1 tablespoon balsamic vinegar
- 1 teaspoon salt
- ½ teaspoon onion powder
- ½ teaspoon garlic powder
- ⅛ teaspoon black pepper

ROMAINE HEARTS
- 6 romaine hearts
- ¼ to ½ cup olive oil
- Salt and black pepper

1. For vinaigrette, whisk cola, white vinegar, canola oil, sugar, ketchup, mustard, balsamic vinegar, 1 teaspoon salt, onion powder, garlic powder and ⅛ teaspoon pepper in medium bowl; set aside.

2. Prepare grill for direct cooking over medium-high heat. Cut romaine hearts in half lengthwise; drizzle with olive oil and sprinkle generously with salt and pepper.

3. Grill about 2 minutes per side or until wilted and lightly charred.

4. Drizzle with vinaigrette. Refrigerate remaining vinaigrette for another use.

Tip

This recipe makes 4 cups of dressing, which is more than you will use on the lettuce. Extra dressing is always great to have on hand for other salads, pasta salads or as a marinade for grilled meats. But if you don't want tons of extra dressing, cut the ingredients in half.

Cola in salad dressing gives it a sweet and tangy twist.

Sides & Casseroles

HORSERADISH SCALLOPED POTATOES
MAKES 4 TO 6 SERVINGS

- ¾ cup milk
- 3 tablespoons horseradish
- 2 pounds Yukon Gold potatoes, peeled
- ¾ cup whipping cream
- 1 teaspoon salt
- ½ teaspoon black pepper
- ½ cup (2 ounces) shredded Swiss cheese

1. Preheat oven to 375°F. Grease 1½-quart baking dish.
2. Combine milk and horseradish in medium microwavable bowl. Microwave on HIGH about 1 minute or just until hot.
3. Cut potatoes into ¼-inch-thick slices; layer slices in prepared baking dish. Stir cream, salt and pepper into milk mixture; pour over potatoes.
4. Cover and bake 40 minutes. Sprinkle with cheese; bake, uncovered, 40 minutes or until bubbly and golden brown.

Horseradish adds a spicy kick to classic creamy scalloped potatoes.

Sides & Casseroles

CURRIED LENTILS WITH FRUIT
MAKES 6 SERVINGS

- 2 quarts water
- 1½ cups dried lentils, rinsed and sorted*
- 1 Granny Smith apple, peeled and chopped
- ¼ cup golden raisins
- ¼ cup plain yogurt
- 1 teaspoon curry powder
- 1 teaspoon salt

Packages of dried lentils occasionally contain grit or tiny stones. Sort through and discard any foreign matter.

1. Combine water and lentils in large saucepan; bring to a boil over high heat. Reduce heat to medium-low. Simmer 20 minutes, stirring occasionally.

2. Stir apple and raisins into saucepan; cook 10 minutes or until lentils are tender. Drain.

3. Place lentil mixture in large bowl; stir in yogurt, curry powder and salt.

Tip
Apples brown easily once they are cut. Sprinkle with lemon or lime juice if not using immediately to prevent browning.

Spice up your lentils with tart apples and curry powder.

Sides & Casseroles

POTATO NUGGET CASSEROLE
MAKES 8 SERVINGS

- 2 pounds frozen potato nuggets
- 1 can (10¾ ounces) condensed cream of celery soup, undiluted
- 1 can (10¾ ounces) condensed cream of mushroom soup, undiluted
- 1 can (10¾ ounces) condensed Cheddar cheese soup, undiluted
- 1 can (about 5 ounces) evaporated milk
- 2 cups (8 ounces) shredded mozzarella cheese
- 2 cups (8 ounces) shredded Cheddar cheese

1. Preheat oven to 350°F. Spread potato nuggets in 13×9-inch baking dish.

2. Mix soups and evaporated milk in large saucepan. Bring to a boil, stirring occasionally. Pour over potatoes; mix until well blended.

3. Bake 45 minutes. Sprinkle cheeses evenly over casserole; bake 5 minutes or until cheeses are melted.

Variation

For a hearty one-dish meal, brown 1 pound of ground beef in a large skillet over medium heat, stirring to break up meat. Stir into the soup mixture.

Turn classic creamy potato casserole on its head with potato nuggets.

Sides & Casseroles

ROASTED BRUSSELS SPROUTS SALAD
MAKES 6 SERVINGS

BRUSSELS SPROUTS
- 1 pound Brussels sprouts, trimmed and halved
- 2 tablespoons olive oil
- ½ teaspoon salt

SALAD
- 2 cups coarsely chopped baby kale
- 2 cups coarsely chopped romaine lettuce
- 1½ cups candied pecans*
- 1 cup halved red grapes
- 1 cup diced cucumbers
- ½ cup dried cranberries
- ½ cup fresh blueberries
- ½ cup chopped red onion
- ¼ cup toasted pumpkin seeds (pepitas)
- 1 container (4 ounces) crumbled goat cheese

DRESSING
- ½ cup olive oil
- 6 tablespoons balsamic vinegar
- 6 tablespoons strawberry jam
- 2 teaspoons Dijon mustard
- 1 teaspoon salt

*Candied or glazed pecans may be found in the produce section of the supermarket with other salad toppings, or they may be found in the snack aisle.

1. For Brussels sprouts, preheat oven to 400°F. Spray large baking sheet with nonstick cooking spray.

2. Combine Brussels sprouts, 2 tablespoons oil and ½ teaspoon salt in medium bowl; toss to coat. Arrange Brussels sprouts in single layer, cut sides down, on prepared baking sheet. Roast 20 minutes or until tender and browned, stirring once halfway through roasting. Cool completely on baking sheet.

3. For salad, combine kale, lettuce, pecans, grapes, cucumbers, cranberries, blueberries, onion and pumpkin seeds in large bowl. Top with Brussels sprouts and cheese.

4. For dressing, whisk ½ cup oil, vinegar, jam, mustard and 1 teaspoon salt in small bowl until well blended. Pour dressing over salad; toss gently to coat.

In addition to a surprising mix of fruit in the salad, the strawberry jam adds a ton of sweet tart flavor to the dressing.

Sides & Casseroles

FRUITY BAKED BEANS
MAKES 6 TO 8 SERVINGS

- 2 tablespoons olive oil
- ¼ cup chopped onion
- 2 cans (16 ounces each) baked beans
- 1 can (about 11 ounces) mandarin oranges, drained
- 1 can (about 8 ounces) pineapple chunks in juice, drained
- ½ cup chopped green bell pepper
- 1 can (about 4 ounces) deviled ham
- ¼ cup ketchup
- 2 tablespoons packed brown sugar
- ½ teaspoon salt (optional)
- Dash hot pepper sauce

1. Preheat oven to 375°F. Heat oil in small skillet over medium heat. Add onion; cook and stir 2 minutes or until translucent.

2. Combine onion, beans, oranges, pineapple, bell pepper, ham, ketchup and brown sugar in large bowl. Taste and stir in salt, if desired; season with hot pepper sauce. Spread mixture in 2-quart baking dish.

3. Bake, uncovered, 30 to 35 minutes or until bubbly.

Canned fruit is a surprisingly delicious addition to canned baked beans.

Sides & Casseroles

KALE SALAD WITH CHERRIES AND AVOCADOS
MAKES 6 TO 8 SERVINGS

- ¼ cup plus 1 teaspoon olive oil, divided
- 3 tablespoons uncooked quinoa
- ¾ teaspoon salt, divided
- 3 tablespoons balsamic vinegar
- 1 tablespoon red wine vinegar
- 1 tablespoon maple syrup
- 2 teaspoons Dijon mustard
- ¼ teaspoon dried oregano
- ⅛ teaspoon black pepper
- 1 large bunch kale (about 1 pound)
- 1 package (5 ounces) dried cherries
- 2 avocados, diced
- ½ cup smoked almonds, chopped

1. Heat 1 teaspoon oil in small saucepan over medium-high heat. Add quinoa; cook and stir 3 to 5 minutes or until quinoa is golden brown and popped. Season with ¼ teaspoon salt. Remove to plate; cool completely.

2. Combine balsamic vinegar, red wine vinegar, maple syrup, mustard, oregano, pepper and remaining ½ teaspoon salt in medium bowl. Whisk in remaining ¼ cup oil until well blended.

3. Place kale in large bowl. Pour dressing over kale; massage dressing into leaves until well blended and kale is slightly softened. Add popped quinoa; stir until well blended. Add cherries, avocados and almonds; toss until blended.

Lightly popped quinoa adds a surprising flavor and crunch to a sweet tart salad.

Sweetened condensed milk and ramen make a surprising treat halfway between a candy bar and a cereal treat.

Sweets

COCONUT ALMOND RAMEN BARS
MAKES 2 TO 3 DOZEN BARS

- 1¼ cups sweetened shredded coconut
- 1 package (3 ounces) ramen noodles, crushed*
- ½ cup slivered almonds, coarsely chopped
- ¾ cup sweetened condensed milk
- ¾ teaspoon vanilla
- ¼ teaspoon salt
- ¾ cup powdered sugar
- 8 ounces chocolate candy coating

*Use any flavor; discard seasoning packet.

1. Line bottom and sides of 13×9-inch baking pan with foil; spray foil with nonstick cooking spray.

2. Heat large nonstick skillet over medium heat. Add coconut, noodles and almonds; cook 3 to 5 minutes or until slightly golden brown, stirring frequently.

3. Combine condensed milk, vanilla and salt in large bowl until well blended. Stir in powdered sugar. Fold in noodle mixture; stir until well blended. Press mixture into prepared pan.

4. Melt chocolate according to package directions. Spread chocolate evenly over noodle mixture. Freeze 15 minutes or until topping is firm. Cut into bars.

Sweets

DEVIL'S FOOD SHEET CAKE
MAKES 12 TO 16 SERVINGS

CAKE
- 1½ cups granulated sugar
- 1½ cups all-purpose flour
- ¾ cup unsweetened cocoa powder
- ½ cup packed brown sugar
- 1½ teaspoons baking soda
- 1½ teaspoons baking powder
- 1 teaspoon salt
- 1 cup buttermilk or milk
- 2 eggs
- ½ cup vegetable oil
- 1 teaspoon vanilla
- 2 teaspoons instant coffee granules or instant espresso powder
- 1 cup boiling water

FROSTING
- 1 package (10 ounces) bittersweet or semisweet chocolate chips
- ¼ teaspoon salt
- 1 can (about 13 ounces) full-fat coconut milk
- 1 teaspoon vanilla
- 2 cups powdered sugar
- Colored decors (optional)

1. Preheat oven to 350°F. Spray 13×9-inch baking pan with nonstick cooking spray or line with parchment paper.

2. For cake, combine granulated sugar, flour, cocoa, brown sugar, baking soda, baking powder and 1 teaspoon salt in large bowl of electric mixer; mix at low speed to blend. Add buttermilk, eggs, oil and 1 teaspoon vanilla; beat at medium speed 2 minutes.

3. Stir instant coffee into boiling water in measuring cup or small bowl until well blended. Add to chocolate mixture; stir until blended. (Batter will be thin.) Pour batter into prepared pan.

4. Bake about 30 minutes or until top appears dry and toothpick inserted into center comes out clean. Cool completely in pan on wire rack.

5. For frosting, place chocolate chips and ¼ teaspoon salt in mixer bowl. Bring coconut milk to a simmer in small saucepan over medium heat, whisking frequently to blend. Pour 1 cup coconut milk over chips; swirl to coat. Let stand 5 minutes. Add 1 teaspoon vanilla; whisk until smooth. Cool to room temperature.*

6. Add powdered sugar; beat on low speed until blended. Increase speed to medium-high; beat 1 to 2 minutes or until frosting is fluffy and smooth. If frosting is too thick, add remaining coconut milk by teaspoonfuls until desired consistency is reached.

7. Spread frosting over cake; sprinkle with decors, if desired.

To frost cake with ganache instead of frosting, spread cooled mixture over top of cake (skip the powdered sugar). For firm ganache, refrigerate until set.

Surprise! Canned coconut milk and chocolate make a quick and tasty frosting.

Sweets

CARROT CUPCAKES
MAKES 12 CUPCAKES

CUPCAKES

- 1½ cups all-purpose flour
- 1 teaspoon baking soda
- 1 teaspoon baking powder
- 1 teaspoon ground cinnamon
- ½ teaspoon salt
- ½ teaspoon ground ginger
- ½ teaspoon ground nutmeg
- ½ teaspoon ground cloves
- 3 eggs
- ½ cup plus 2 tablespoons vegetable oil
- ½ cup granulated sugar
- ¼ cup plus 2 tablespoons cola beverage
- ¼ cup packed brown sugar
- ¾ cup grated carrots

CREAM CHEESE FROSTING

- 1 package (8 ounces) cream cheese, softened
- 1¼ cups powdered sugar
- 1 tablespoon milk, plus additional as needed

1. Preheat oven to 350°F. Line 12 standard (2½-inch) muffin cups with paper baking cups or spray with nonstick cooking spray.

2. Whisk flour, baking soda, baking powder, cinnamon, salt, ginger, nutmeg and cloves in medium bowl.

3. Combine eggs, oil, granulated sugar, cola and brown sugar in large bowl; mix well. Stir in flour mixture just until blended. Add carrots; stir until blended. Spoon batter evenly into prepared muffin cups.

4. Bake 15 minutes or until toothpick inserted into centers comes out clean. Cool in pan 5 minutes. Remove from pan to wire racks; cool completely.

5. For frosting, beat cream cheese, powdered sugar and 1 tablespoon milk in large bowl with electric mixer at medium speed until light and creamy, adding additional milk until frosting is desired consistency. Spread frosting over cupcakes; garnish as desired.

Cola adds a spicy tang to classic carrot cupcakes.

Sweets

CHOCOLATE CAKE MILKSHAKE
MAKES 1 SERVING (2 CUPS)

- 1 slice (⅛ of cake) Rich Chocolate Cake (recipe follows)
- ½ cup milk
- 2 scoops vanilla ice cream (about 1 cup total)

1. Prepare and frost Rich Chocolate Cake.
2. Combine milk, ice cream and cake slice in blender; blend just until cake is incorporated but texture of shake is not completely smooth.

RICH CHOCOLATE CAKE

- 1 package (about 15 ounces) devil's food cake mix
- 1 cup cold water
- 1 cup mayonnaise
- 3 eggs
- 1½ containers (16 ounces each) chocolate frosting

1. Preheat oven to 350°F. Spray two 9-inch round cake pans with nonstick cooking spray.
2. Beat cake mix, water, mayonnaise and eggs in large bowl with electric mixer at low speed 30 seconds. Beat at medium speed 2 minutes. Pour batter into prepared pans.
3. Bake 25 minutes or until toothpick inserted into centers comes out clean. Cool in pans 10 minutes. Remove to wire racks; cool completely.
4. Fill and frost cake with chocolate frosting.

The not-so-secret ingredient in this milkshake? A piece of frosted chocolate cake!

Sweets

ICE CREAM SANDWICHES
MAKES 8 SANDWICHES

CANDIED BACON
- 8 to 10 slices bacon
- ¼ to ½ cup packed brown sugar

SANDWICHES
- 1 package (about 15 ounces) chocolate cake mix with pudding in the mix
- 2 eggs
- ¼ cup warm water
- 3 tablespoons butter, melted
- 2 cups vanilla ice cream, softened

1. For candied bacon, preheat oven to 400°F. Line 15×10-inch rimmed baking sheet with foil. Coat both sides of each strip of bacon with brown sugar. Bake 18 to 20 minutes or until crispy, turning after 10 minutes.

2. *Reduce oven temperature to 350°F.* Line 13×9-inch baking pan with foil; spray foil with nonstick cooking spray.

3. Combine cake mix, eggs, water and butter in large bowl; beat with electric mixer at low speed until well blended. (Dough will be thick and sticky.) Press dough evenly into prepared pan; prick surface all over with fork (about 40 times).

4. Bake 20 minutes or until toothpick inserted into center comes out clean. Cool in pan on wire rack.

5. Cut cookie in half crosswise; remove one half from pan. Spread ice cream evenly over cookie half remaining in pan. Top with second half.

6. Freeze at least 4 hours. Cut into eight equal pieces. Crumble bacon; dip sides of sandwiches in candied bacon. Wrap sandwiches in parchment paper; freeze until ready to serve.

Note
If the ice cream is too hard to scoop easily, microwave on HIGH 10 seconds to soften.

Candied bacon makes a sweet and salty garnish for simple ice cream sandwiches.

Sweets

MARBLED COOKIE BROWNIE
MAKES 9 TO 12 SERVINGS

- 1 cup plus 1 tablespoon all-purpose flour
- ½ teaspoon baking soda
- ½ teaspoon salt
- ½ cup (1 stick) butter, softened
- ½ cup packed brown sugar
- ¼ cup granulated sugar
- 1 egg
- ½ teaspoon vanilla
- 1 cup milk chocolate chunks or chips
- 1 package (18 to 19 ounces) brownie mix, plus ingredients to prepare mix

1. Preheat oven to 350°F. Line 9-inch square baking pan with parchment paper; spray paper with nonstick cooking spray.

2. For cookies, whisk flour, baking soda and salt in small bowl. Beat butter, brown sugar and granulated sugar in large bowl with electric mixer at medium speed about 3 minutes or until light and fluffy, scraping down side of bowl occasionally. Add egg; beat until well blended. Beat in vanilla. Gradually add flour mixture; beat at low speed just until blended. Stir in chocolate chunks. Cover and refrigerate dough while preparing brownies.

3. Prepare brownie mix according to package directions. Spread batter in prepared pan; smooth top. Scoop out eight 1½-tablespoon balls of cookie dough; roll into smooth, round balls. (Reserve remaining cookie dough for another use.) Scatter cookie dough balls over brownie batter; press down gently to push cookie dough into brownie batter.

4. Bake 25 minutes, then cover loosely with foil to prevent cookies from becoming too brown. Bake 13 minutes or until brownies are firm, edges begin to come away from side of pan and toothpick inserted into center comes out clean. Cool in pan on wire rack 10 minutes. Cut into bars. Serve warm or at room temperature.

Brownie batter is the secret ingredient you never knew you needed for chocolate chip cookies.

Sweets

DOUBLE CHOCOLATE BUNDT CAKE
MAKES 12 SERVINGS

- 2 cups all-purpose flour
- 1 cup sugar
- ¼ cup unsweetened cocoa powder
- 1½ teaspoons baking powder
- 1½ teaspoons baking soda
- ¼ teaspoon salt
- 1 cup mayonnaise
- 1 cup hot coffee
- 2 teaspoons vanilla
- ¼ cup whipping cream
- ½ cup semisweet chocolate chips

1. Preheat oven to 350°F. Grease and flour 10-inch bundt pan.

2. Whisk flour, sugar, cocoa, baking powder, baking soda and salt in large bowl. Stir in mayonnaise, coffee and vanilla until batter is smooth. Pour into prepared pan.

3. Bake 30 minutes or until toothpick inserted near center comes out clean. Cool in pan on wire rack 10 minutes. Invert onto wire rack or cake plate; cool completely.

4. For glaze, bring cream to a simmer in small saucepan over low heat. Remove from heat. Add chocolate chips; stir until melted and smooth. Drizzle glaze over cake.

Mayonnaise and hot coffee work together in this cake to make it extra moist and delicious.

Sweets

CHOCOLATE AVOCADO PUDDING
MAKES 4 TO 6 SERVINGS

- 3 ripe avocados, peeled and pitted
- ¼ cup plus 2 tablespoons unsweetened cocoa powder
- ¼ cup plus 2 tablespoons packed brown sugar
- ¼ cup unsweetened nondairy milk (almond, oat, rice or soy)
- 2 teaspoons vanilla
- ¼ teaspoon salt
- ½ cup semisweet chocolate chips, melted

1. Combine avocado, cocoa, brown sugar, nondairy milk, vanilla and salt in food processor; process 2 minutes. Add melted chocolate; process 2 to 3 minutes or until very smooth and thick.
2. Serve immediately or refrigerate until ready to serve.

Avocados blend seamlessly into this creamy vegan chocolate pudding.

Sweets

PUMPKIN BARS
MAKES 2 TO 3 DOZEN BARS

CAKE
- 1 cup all-purpose flour
- 1 cup whole wheat flour
- ¾ cup granulated sugar
- 1½ teaspoons baking powder
- 1½ teaspoons ground cinnamon
- 1 teaspoon baking soda
- 1 teaspoon salt
- ½ teaspoon ground nutmeg
- ½ teaspoon ground ginger
- 1 can (15 ounces) pumpkin purée
- 2 eggs
- ¼ cup canola oil
- 1 container (2½ ounces) puréed baby food prunes
- 2 tablespoons packed brown sugar
- 2 tablespoons molasses

FROSTING
- 1 package (8 ounces) cream cheese, softened
- 2 tablespoons granulated sugar
- ½ cup whipped topping
- ½ cup mini chocolate chips

1. Preheat oven to 350°F. Spray 13×9-inch pan with nonstick cooking spray or line with parchment paper.

2. Whisk flours, ¾ cup granulated sugar, baking powder, cinnamon, baking soda, salt, nutmeg and ginger in medium bowl.

3. Beat pumpkin, eggs, oil, prune purée, brown sugar and molasses in large bowl until well blended. Add dry ingredients; stir just until blended. Spread batter evenly in prepared pan.

4. Bake 20 to 25 minutes or until toothpick inserted into center comes out clean. Cool completely in pan on wire rack.

5. For frosting, beat cream cheese and 2 tablespoons granulated sugar in large bowl with electric mixer at medium speed until smooth. Fold in whipped topping with spatula until well blended. Spread frosting onto cooled cake; sprinkle with chocolate chips. Cut into bars to serve.

Baby food is this cake's secret to a moist and tender crumb.

Sweets

CHOCOLATE MINT COOKIE PIE
MAKES 8 TO 10 SERVINGS

- 30 marshmallows
- ½ cup milk
- 4 ounces bittersweet chocolate, chopped
- 2 ounces unsweetened chocolate, chopped
- ½ teaspoon mint extract
- 1½ cups whipping cream
- 1 (6-ounce) chocolate crumb pie crust
- 1 container (8 ounces) thawed frozen whipped topping
- 12 chocolate mint sandwich cookies, chopped

1. Combine marshmallows and milk in medium saucepan; cook over medium heat 7 minutes or until melted and smooth, stirring constantly. Remove from heat; stir in chopped chocolate and mint extract until melted and smooth.

2. Whip cream in large bowl with electric mixer at high speed until stiff peaks form. Fold one fourth of whipped cream into chocolate mixture just until lightened. Fold chocolate mixture into remaining whipped cream until blended. Spread evenly in crust.

3. Spread whipped topping over top of pie; sprinkle with cookie pieces. Refrigerate at least 3 hours or overnight.

This no-bake pie gets its creaminess from melted marshmallows.

Sweets

CHOCOLATE RAMEN FUDGE
MAKES 18 SERVINGS

- 1 package (about 11 ounces) semisweet chocolate chips
- 1 can (14 ounces) sweetened condensed milk
- 1 package (3 ounces) ramen noodles, crumbled*
- 2 tablespoons butter, softened
- 1 teaspoon vanilla

*Use any flavor; discard seasoning packet.

1. Line 8-inch square baking pan with foil, extending foil over edges of pan.
2. Place chocolate chips in medium microwavable bowl. Microwave on HIGH 1 minute; stir. Repeat heating and stirring at 30-second intervals until completely melted. Add condensed milk, crumbled noodles, butter and vanilla; stir until well blended.
3. Pour mixture into prepared pan; spread into even layer. Refrigerate 1 hour or until firm.
4. Remove fudge from pan; peel off foil and cut into squares.

The crispy crunchy secret to this tasty fudge is uncooked ramen noodles.

Sweets

FUDGY FROSTED BROWNIES
MAKES 12 TO 16 BROWNIES

BROWNIES

- 4 ounces unsweetened chocolate, chopped
- ½ cup (1 stick) butter, cut into pieces
- 1 cup granulated sugar
- ¾ cup packed dark brown sugar
- 2 eggs
- 2 tablespoons cola beverage
- 1 teaspoon vanilla
- ½ teaspoon salt
- 1 cup all-purpose flour

COLA FROSTING

- ¼ cup (½ stick) butter, cut into pieces
- 3 tablespoons cola beverage
- 2 tablespoons cocoa powder
- 1⅓ cups powdered sugar, sifted
- ½ teaspoon vanilla

1. Preheat oven to 350°F. Line bottom and sides of 8-inch pan with foil; spray foil with nonstick cooking spray.

2. Combine chocolate and ½ cup butter in medium heavy saucepan. Cook over low heat until chocolate and butter are melted, stirring constantly. Stir in granulated sugar and brown sugar until blended. Add eggs, one at a time. Stir in 2 tablespoons cola, 1 teaspoon vanilla and salt. Stir in flour until blended. Pour batter into prepared pan.

3. Bake 35 to 40 minutes or until toothpick inserted into center comes out clean. Cool completely in pan on wire rack.

4. Meanwhile for frosting, heat ½ cup butter, 3 tablespoons cola and cocoa in medium heavy saucepan over medium-low heat, stirring until butter melts. Remove from heat; whisk in powdered sugar and ½ teaspoon vanilla. Spread over brownies; cut into bars.

Cola adds a hint of something special to deliciously chocolatey brownies.

Sweets

LEFTOVER CANDY ICE CREAM PIE
MAKES 10 SERVINGS

Brown Sugar Crumb Crust (recipe follows)
2 cups vanilla ice cream
½ cup chocolate sauce
8 snack-size chocolate candy bars,* chopped
2 cups chocolate ice cream
¾ cup whipping cream

Use your favorite leftover Halloween candy bars or use 3 to 4 full-size candy bars.

1. Prepare Brown Sugar Crumb Crust.
2. Let vanilla ice cream stand at room temperature about 5 minutes or just until softened; spread evenly over crust. Drizzle with ¼ cup chocolate sauce; sprinkle with half of chopped candy bars. Freeze 1½ hours or until firm.
3. Let chocolate ice cream stand at room temperature about 5 minutes or just until softened; spread evenly over chopped candy bars. Drizzle with remaining ¼ cup chocolate sauce. Freeze 6 hours or until firm.
4. Let pie stand in refrigerator 20 minutes to soften before serving.
5. Whip cream in large bowl with electric mixer fitted with wire whip at high speed 2 to 3 minutes or until stiff peaks form. Spread whipped cream over pie; sprinkle with remaining chopped candy bars.

Brown Sugar Crumb Crust

Preheat oven to 350°F. Combine 1¼ cups graham cracker crumbs, 2 tablespoons packed brown sugar and ⅓ cup melted butter in large bowl; mix well. Press onto bottom and up side of 9-inch pie plate. Bake 8 to 10 minutes or until edges are golden brown. Cool completely on wire rack.

The secret ingredient in this creamy pie is any leftover candy you want! Surprise family and friends with any candy you'd like to add.

Index

A
Almond Chicken Salad Sandwich, 40
Almonds
    Coconut Almond Ramen Bars, 163
    Pumpkin Granola, 6
    Tomato and Brie Noodles, 120
Artichokes
    Farro, Mozzarella and Pepperoni Salad, 135
    Tuna Artichoke Cups, 66
Avocado
    Chocolate Avocado Pudding, 176
    Kale Salad with Cherries and Avocados, 160

B
Bacon
    Bacon and Egg Breakfast Casserole, 20
    Bacon Broccoli Slaw, 144
    Ice Cream Sandwiches, 170
Bacon and Egg Breakfast Casserole, 20
Bacon Broccoli Slaw, 144
Baked Pumpkin Oatmeal, 26
Balsamic Chicken, 108
Banana Bread Waffles with Cinnamon Butter, 28
Bavarian Pretzel Sandwiches, 50
BBQ Portobellos, 40
Beans
    Black Bean Dip, 72
    Fruity Baked Beans, 158
    Jalapeño Beans, 142
Beef
    Meatball Sliders, 64
    Ramen Tamale Pie, 138
Beer
    Jalapeño Beans, 142
Bell Peppers
    Farro, Mozzarella and Pepperoni Salad, 135
    Fruity Baked Beans, 158
    Mock Fried Rice, 126
    Pasta Primavera with Ricotta, 122
    Skillet Lasagna with Vegetables, 94
    Squash Lasagna, 104

Bell Peppers *(continued)*
    Turkey Meat Loaf, 102
    Vegetable and Cheese Sandwiches, 35
Biscuit Baking Mix
    Biscuit-Topped Chicken Pot Pie, 96
    Cherry Scones with Strawberry Butter, 30
Biscuit-Topped Chicken Pot Pie, 96
Black Bean Dip, 72
Breads
    Cherry Scones with Strawberry Butter, 30
    Marbled Banana Bread, 18
    Surprise Corn Muffins, 88
    Three-Ingredient Bagels, 22
Breakfast Sausage Monkey Muffins, 5
Broccoli
    Bacon Broccoli Slaw, 144
    Mock Fried Rice, 126
    Surprise Corn Muffins, 88
    Vegetable Pizza Primavera, 56
Brown Sugar Crumb Crust, 186
Brownies and Bars
    Coconut Almond Ramen Bars, 163
    Fudgy Frosted Brownies, 184
    Marbled Cookie Brownie, 172
Buffalo Cauliflower Bites, 76

C
Cake Mix
    Graham Pancakes, 14
    Ice Cream Sandwiches, 170
    Rich Chocolate Cake, 168
Cakes and Cupcakes
    Carrot Cupcakes, 166
    Chocolate Cake Milkshake, 168
    Devil's Food Sheet Cake, 164
    Double Chocolate Bundt Cake, 174
    Pumpkin Bars, 178
    Rich Chocolate Cake, 168
Carrot Cupcakes, 166
Casseroles
    Bacon and Egg Breakfast Casserole, 20
    Egg and Green Chile Rice Casserole, 32

Casseroles *(continued)*
    Fruited Corn Pudding, 146
    Fruity Baked Beans, 158
    Horseradish Scalloped Potatoes, 150
    Potato Nugget Casserole, 154
    Pumpkin Mac and Cheese, 124
    Ramen Tamale Pie, 138
    Squash Lasagna, 104
Cauliflower
    Bacon and Egg Breakfast Casserole, 20
    Buffalo Cauliflower Bites, 76
    Cauliflower Mac and Gouda, 128
    Cauliflower Picnic Salad, 140
    Chorizo Quesadillas, 38
    Garlic and Onion Sheet Pan Pizza, 36
    Roasted Tomato Quiche, 16
    Sweet-Spicy Breaded Cauliflower, 61
    Tofu Cauliflower Fried Rice, 92
Cauliflower Mac and Gouda, 128
Cauliflower Picnic Salad, 140
Cheese
    Bacon and Egg Breakfast Casserole, 20
    Black Bean Dip, 72
    Breakfast Sausage Monkey Muffins, 5
    Cauliflower Mac and Gouda, 128
    Cheese Ravioli with Pumpkin Sauce, 112
    Chorizo Quesadillas, 38
    Crunchy Cheese Ball with Strawberry-Pepper Sauce, 84
    Egg and Green Chile Rice Casserole, 32
    Eggplant Pizzas, 62
    Farro, Mozzarella and Pepperoni Salad, 135
    Garlic and Onion Sheet Pan Pizza, 36
    Hearty Veggie Sandwich, 48
    Horseradish Scalloped Potatoes, 150
    Margherita Pizza with Quinoa Crust, 42
    Meatball Sliders, 64
    Pasta Primavera with Ricotta, 122
    Potato Nugget Casserole, 154

Index

Cheese *(continued)*
- Pumpkin Mac and Cheese, 124
- Pumpkin Risotto, 136
- Quick and Easy Arancini, 74
- Ramen Alfredo, 132
- Ramen Tamale Pie, 138
- Roasted Brussels Sprouts Salad, 156
- Roasted Tomato Quiche, 16
- Skillet Lasagna with Vegetables, 94
- Spaghetti and Beets Aglio e Olio, 115
- Squash Lasagna, 104
- Summer Vegetable Pizza, 52
- Tomato and Brie Noodles, 120
- Turkey Dinner Quesadilla, 44
- Vegetable and Cheese Sandwiches, 35
- Vegetable Pizza Primavera, 56
- Warm Salsa and Goat Cheese Dip, 80

Cheese Ravioli with Pumpkin Sauce, 112
Cherry Scones with Strawberry Butter, 30

Chicken
- Almond Chicken Salad Sandwich, 46
- Balsamic Chicken, 108
- Biscuit-Topped Chicken Pot Pie, 96
- Chicken in a Blanket, 78
- Hot Sweet Mustard Chicken, 106
- Jalapeño-Lime Chicken, 100
- Sweet Sticky Pineapple Chicken with Rice, 110
- Tangy Barbecue Chicken Skewers, 82

Chicken in a Blanket, 78

Chocolate
- Chocolate Avocado Pudding, 176
- Chocolate Cake Milkshake, 168
- Chocolate Mint Cookie Pie, 180
- Chocolate Ramen Fudge, 182
- Coconut Almond Ramen Bars, 163
- Devil's Food Sheet Cake, 164
- Double Chocolate Bundt Cake, 174

Chocolate *(continued)*
- Fudgy Frosted Brownies, 184
- Ice Cream Sandwiches, 170
- Leftover Candy Ice Cream Pie, 186
- Marbled Banana Bread, 18
- Marbled Cookie Brownie, 172
- Pumpkin Bars, 178
- Rich Chocolate Cake, 168

Chocolate Avocado Pudding, 176
Chocolate Cake Milkshake, 168
Chocolate Mint Cookie Pie, 180
Chocolate Ramen Fudge, 182
Chorizo Quesadillas, 38
Cinnamon-Sugar Waffled Bagels, 8
Coconut Almond Ramen Bars, 163

Coconut and Coconut Milk
- Coconut Almond Ramen Bars, 163
- Devil's Food Sheet Cake, 164

Cola
- Balsamic Chicken, 108
- Black Bean Dip, 72
- Carrot Cupcakes, 166
- Fudgy Frosted Brownies, 184
- Grilled Romaine with Tangy Vinaigrette, 148
- Sweet Sticky Pineapple Chicken with Rice, 110

Corn
- Fruited Corn Pudding, 146
- Ramen Tamale Pie, 138

Cranberry
- Baked Pumpkin Oatmeal, 26
- Fruited Corn Pudding, 146
- Meatball Sliders, 64
- Pumpkin Granola, 6
- Roasted Brussels Sprouts Salad, 156
- Turkey Dinner Quesadilla, 44

Crunchy Cheese Ball with Strawberry-Pepper Sauce, 84
Curried Lentils with Fruit, 152

D
Devil's Food Sheet Cake, 164

Dips and Spreads
- Black Bean Dip, 72
- Crunchy Cheese Ball with Strawberry-Pepper Sauce, 84

Dips and Spreads *(continued)*
- Savory Pumpkin Hummus, 68
- Warm Salsa and Goat Cheese Dip, 80
- Double Chocolate Bundt Cake, 174

Dough, Refrigerated and Frozen
- Breakfast Sausage Monkey Muffins, 5
- Chicken in a Blanket, 78

E
Egg and Green Chile Rice Casserole, 32

Egg Dishes
- Bacon and Egg Breakfast Casserole, 20
- Cauliflower Picnic Salad, 140
- Egg and Green Chile Rice Casserole, 32
- Fruited Corn Pudding, 146
- Quinoa Breakfast Fried "Rice," 24
- Roasted Tomato Quiche, 16
- Shortcut Spanish Tortilla, 86

Eggplant
- Eggplant Pizzas, 62
- Squash Lasagna, 104
- Summer Vegetable Pizza, 52

Eggplant Pizzas, 62

F
Farro, Mozzarella and Pepperoni Salad, 135
Fruited Corn Pudding, 146
Fruity Baked Beans, 158
Fruity Whole-Grain Cereal, 12
Fudgy Frosted Brownies, 184

G
Garlic and Onion Sheet Pan Pizza, 36
Graham Pancakes, 14

Grapes
- Almond Chicken Salad Sandwich, 46
- Roasted Brussels Sprouts Salad, 156

Grilled Romaine with Tangy Vinaigrette, 148

Index

H
Ham
  Bavarian Pretzel Sandwiches, 50
  Fruity Baked Beans, 158
Hearty Veggie Sandwich, 48
Horseradish Scalloped Potatoes, 150
Hot Dog Sloppy Joe Sandwiches, 58
Hot Sweet Mustard Chicken, 106

I
Ice Cream
  Chocolate Cake Milkshake, 168
  Ice Cream Sandwiches, 170
  Leftover Candy Ice Cream Pie, 186
Ice Cream Sandwiches, 170

J
Jalapeño Beans, 142
Jalapeño-Lime Chicken, 100

K
Kale
  Kale Salad with Cherries and Avocados, 160
  Roasted Brussels Sprouts Salad, 156
Kale Salad with Cherries and Avocados, 160

L
Leftover Candy Ice Cream Pie, 186
Lentil Ragù, 116
Lentils
  Curried Lentils with Fruit, 152
  Lentil Ragù, 116
Linguine with Sun-Dried Tomato Pesto, 130

M
Marbled Banana Bread, 18
Marbled Cookie Brownie, 172
Margherita Pizza with Quinoa Crust, 42
Meatball Sliders, 64
Mock Fried Rice, 126

Muffin Tin Recipes
  Breakfast Sausage Monkey Muffins, 5
  Quick and Easy Arancini, 74
  Surprise Corn Muffins, 88
  Tuna Artichoke Cups, 66
Mushrooms
  BBQ Portobellos, 40
  Hearty Veggie Sandwich, 48
  Lentil Ragù, 116
  Squash Lasagna, 104
  Veggie "Meatballs," 98
  Wing-Style Fried Mushrooms, 70

O
Oats
  Baked Pumpkin Oatmeal, 26
  Fruity Whole-Grain Cereal, 12
  Pumpkin Granola, 6
  Turkey Meat Loaf, 102

P
Pasta and Noodle Dishes
  Cauliflower Mac and Gouda, 128
  Cheese Ravioli with Pumpkin Sauce, 112
  Lentil Ragù, 116
  Linguine with Sun-Dried Tomato Pesto, 130
  Mock Fried Rice, 126
  Pasta Primavera with Ricotta, 122
  Pumpkin Mac and Cheese, 124
  Ramen Tamale Pie, 138
  Sausage Spaghetti, 118
  Skillet Lasagna with Vegetables, 94
  Spaghetti and Beets Aglio e Olio, 115
  Tomato and Brie Noodles, 120
Pasta Primavera with Ricotta, 122
Peas
  Pasta Primavera with Ricotta, 122
  Quick and Easy Arancini, 74
  Quinoa Breakfast Fried "Rice," 24
  Tofu Cauliflower Fried Rice, 92
Pepperoni: Farro, Mozzarella and Pepperoni Salad, 146
Pesto Turkey Meatballs, 91

Pies
  Brown Sugar Crumb Crust, 186
  Chocolate Mint Cookie Pie, 180
  Leftover Candy Ice Cream Pie, 186
Pineapple
  Fruity Baked Beans, 158
  Sweet Sticky Pineapple Chicken with Rice, 110
Pizza
  Eggplant Pizzas, 62
  Garlic and Onion Sheet Pan Pizza, 36
  Margherita Pizza with Quinoa Crust, 42
  Summer Vegetable Pizza, 52
  Vegetable Pizza Primavera, 56
Potato Nugget Casserole, 154
Potatoes
  Horseradish Scalloped Potatoes, 150
  Potato Nugget Casserole, 154
Pumpkin
  Baked Pumpkin Oatmeal, 26
  Cheese Ravioli with Pumpkin Sauce, 112
  Pumpkin Bars, 178
  Pumpkin Granola, 6
  Pumpkin Mac and Cheese, 124
  Pumpkin Risotto, 136
  Savory Pumpkin Hummus, 68
Pumpkin Bars, 178
Pumpkin Granola, 6
Pumpkin Mac and Cheese, 124
Pumpkin Risotto, 136

Q
Quesadillas
  Chorizo Quesadillas, 38
  Turkey Dinner Quesadilla, 44
Quick and Easy Arancini, 74
Quinoa
  Margherita Pizza with Quinoa Crust, 42
  Quinoa Breakfast Fried "Rice," 24
  Kale Salad with Cherries and Avocados, 160
Quinoa Breakfast Fried "Rice," 24

Index

R
Ramen Alfredo, 132
Ramen Noodles
    Bacon Broccoli Slaw, 144
    Chocolate Ramen Fudge, 182
    Coconut Almond Ramen Bars, 163
    Crunchy Cheese Ball with Strawberry-Pepper Sauce, 84
    Mock Fried Rice, 126
    Ramen Alfredo, 132
    Ramen Tamale Pie, 138
    Twisted Cinnamon French Toast, 10
Ramen Tamale Pie, 138
Rice
    Egg and Green Chile Rice Casserole, 32
    Fruity Whole-Grain Cereal, 12
    Pumpkin Risotto, 136
    Quick and Easy Arancini, 74
    Sweet Sticky Pineapple Chicken with Rice, 110
Rich Chocolate Cake, 168
Roasted Brussels Sprouts Salad, 156
Roasted Tomato Quiche, 16

S
Sandwiches
    Almond Chicken Salad Sandwich, 46
    Bavarian Pretzel Sandwiches, 50
    BBQ Portobellos, 40
    Hearty Veggie Sandwich, 48
    Hot Dog Sloppy Joe Sandwiches, 58
    Meatball Sliders, 64
    Vegetable and Cheese Sandwiches, 35
    Veggie-Packed Turkey Burgers, 54
Sausage
    Breakfast Sausage Monkey Muffins, 5
    Chorizo Quesadillas, 38
    Sausage Spaghetti, 118
    Skillet Lasagna with Vegetables, 94
    Squash Lasagna, 104
Sausage Spaghetti, 118
Savory Pumpkin Hummus, 68
Shortcut Spanish Tortilla, 86
Skillet Lasagna with Vegetables, 94
Spaghetti and Beets Aglio e Olio, 115
Spinach
    Hearty Veggie Sandwich, 48
    Turkey Dinner Quesadilla, 44
Spiralizer Recipes
    Pasta Primavera with Ricotta, 122
    Spaghetti and Beets Aglio e Olio, 115
    Squash Lasagna, 104
Strawberry
    Crunchy Cheese Ball with Strawberry-Pepper Sauce, 84
    Roasted Brussels Sprouts Salad, 156
    Summer Vegetable Pizza, 52
    Surprise Corn Muffins, 88
    Sweet Sticky Pineapple Chicken with Rice, 110
    Sweet-Spicy Breaded Cauliflower, 61

T
Tangy Barbecue Chicken Skewers, 82
Three-Ingredient Bagels, 22
Tofu Cauliflower Fried Rice, 92
Tomato and Brie Noodles, 120
Tomatoes
    Lentil Ragù, 116
    Pesto Turkey Meatballs, 91
    Ramen Tamale Pie, 138
    Roasted Tomato Quiche, 16
    Squash Lasagna, 104
    Summer Vegetable Pizza, 52
    Tomato and Brie Noodles, 120
    Veggie "Meatballs," 98
    Warm Salsa and Goat Cheese Dip, 80
Tomatoes, Sun-Dried
    Linguine with Sun-Dried Tomato Pesto, 130
    Veggie "Meatballs," 98
Tortillas and Tortilla Chips
    Chorizo Quesadillas, 38
    Turkey Dinner Quesadilla, 44
    Warm Salsa and Goat Cheese Dip, 80
Tuna Artichoke Cups, 66
Turkey
    Pesto Turkey Meatballs, 91
    Skillet Lasagna with Vegetables, 94
    Turkey Dinner Quesadilla, 44
    Turkey Meat Loaf, 102
    Veggie-Packed Turkey Burgers, 54
Turkey Dinner Quesadilla, 44
Turkey Meat Loaf, 102
Twisted Cinnamon French Toast, 10

V
Vegetable and Cheese Sandwiches, 35
Vegetable Pizza Primavera, 56
Veggie "Meatballs," 98
Veggie-Packed Turkey Burgers, 54

W
Waffle Iron Recipes
    Banana Bread Waffles with Cinnamon Butter, 28
    Cinnamon-Sugar Waffled Bagels, 8
Warm Salsa and Goat Cheese Dip, 80
Wing-Style Fried Mushrooms, 70

Z
Zucchini
    Hearty Veggie Sandwich, 48
    Pasta Primavera with Ricotta, 122
    Pesto Turkey Meatballs, 91
    Skillet Lasagna with Vegetables, 94
    Squash Lasagna, 104
    Summer Vegetable Pizza, 52
    Turkey Meat Loaf, 102
    Vegetable and Cheese Sandwiches, 35
    Veggie "Meatballs," 98
    Veggie-Packed Turkey Burgers, 54

Metric Conversion Chart

VOLUME MEASUREMENTS (dry)

1/8 teaspoon = 0.5 mL
1/4 teaspoon = 1 mL
1/2 teaspoon = 2 mL
3/4 teaspoon = 4 mL
1 teaspoon = 5 mL
1 tablespoon = 15 mL
2 tablespoons = 30 mL
1/4 cup = 60 mL
1/3 cup = 75 mL
1/2 cup = 125 mL
2/3 cup = 150 mL
3/4 cup = 175 mL
1 cup = 250 mL
2 cups = 1 pint = 500 mL
3 cups = 750 mL
4 cups = 1 quart = 1 L

VOLUME MEASUREMENTS (fluid)

1 fluid ounce (2 tablespoons) = 30 mL
4 fluid ounces (1/2 cup) = 125 mL
8 fluid ounces (1 cup) = 250 mL
12 fluid ounces (1 1/2 cups) = 375 mL
16 fluid ounces (2 cups) = 500 mL

WEIGHTS (mass)

1/2 ounce = 15 g
1 ounce = 30 g
3 ounces = 90 g
4 ounces = 120 g
8 ounces = 225 g
10 ounces = 285 g
12 ounces = 360 g
16 ounces = 1 pound = 450 g

DIMENSIONS

1/16 inch = 2 mm
1/8 inch = 3 mm
1/4 inch = 6 mm
1/2 inch = 1.5 cm
3/4 inch = 2 cm
1 inch = 2.5 cm

OVEN TEMPERATURES

250°F = 120°C
275°F = 140°C
300°F = 150°C
325°F = 160°C
350°F = 180°C
375°F = 190°C
400°F = 200°C
425°F = 220°C
450°F = 230°C

BAKING PAN SIZES

Utensil	Size in Inches/Quarts	Metric Volume	Size in Centimeters
Baking or Cake Pan (square or rectangular)	8×8×2 9×9×2 12×8×2 13×9×2	2 L 2.5 L 3 L 3.5 L	20×20×5 23×23×5 30×20×5 33×23×5
Loaf Pan	8×4×3 9×5×3	1.5 L 2 L	20×10×7 23×13×7
Round Layer Cake Pan	8×1 1/2 9×1 1/2	1.2 L 1.5 L	20×4 23×4
Pie Plate	8×1 1/4 9×1 1/4	750 mL 1 L	20×3 23×3
Baking Dish or Casserole	1 quart 1 1/2 quart 2 quart	1 L 1.5 L 2 L	— — —